WOOD PELLET GRILL
101

Everything You Need to Know to Be the Master
of Your Wood Pellet Grill.
With Dessert Section!

Phil Robson

Contents

INTRODUCTION   5

Do I Need a Wood Pellet Smoker-Grill?   5

Trendy Models   5

Temperature Handling   7

To Smoke or To Grill?   8

CHAPTER 1. STARTERS   11

1.1 Spicy & Smoky Cashews   11

1.2. Asian Jumbo Shrimps   11

1.3 Shrimp Stuffed Jalapeños   11

1.4 Garlic Mozzarella Bread   12

1.5 Tennessee Whiskey Bacon   12

1.6 Spiced Jalapeño Balls   13

1.7 Wild Boar Sausage   13

1.8 Southern Stuffed Peppers   13

1.9 Grilled Chicken Legs with Spicy Salsa   14

1.10 Bacon & Cheddar Baby Potatoes   15

1.11 Spicy Nachos Dip   15

1.12 Red Onion Jam, Duck Confit & Goat Cheese Croutons   16

CHAPTER 2. VEGETABLES   17

2.1 Mashed Smoky Potatoes   17

2.2 Caesar Salad on the Grill   17

2.3. Smoked Mediterranean Potato Salad   17

2.4 Potato & Scallion Salad   18

2.5 Skillet Roasted Vegetables   18

2.6 Grilled Bacon & Green Beans   19

2.7 Garlic Herbed Potato Wedges   19

2.8 Grilled Cabbage with Bacon Mustard Vinaigrette   19

2.9 Grilled Beet Salad with Bacon   20

2.10 Grilled Lettuce Salad   20

2.11 Spiced Carrot Salad with Pomegranate Relish   21

2.12 Vermouth Grilled Root Vegetables   21

CHAPTER 3. LAMB   23

3.1 Roasted Lamb Leg   23

3.2 Braised Lamb Shank   23

3.3 Lamb Kebabs   24

3.4 BBQ Lamb Pocket with Tzatziki   24

3.5 Smoked Lamb Sausage   25

3.6 Special Grilled Lamb Burgers   25

3.7 Pulled Lamb Shoulder   26

3.8 Lamb Stew   27

3.9 Irish Braised Lamb   27

3.10 Lamb Chops with Mediterranean Sauce   28

3.11 Lamb Chops with Mango Chutney   28

3.12 Grilled Lamb Rack   29

CHAPTER 4. TURKEY   30

4.1. Brie Stuffed Turkey Burgers   30

4.2 Thanksgiving Smoked Turkey   30

4.3 Smoked Turkey Legs   31

4.4 Cajun Butter Spatchcocked Turkey   31

4.5 Bacon Lattice Turkey   31

4.6 Pepper & Onion Turkey Burgers   32

4.7 Mayonnaise & Herbs Turkey   32

4.8 Smoked Turkey Jerky   33

4.9 Drunken Turkey Legs   33

4.10 Turkey Gravy on the Grill   34

4.11 Bacon Stuffed Turkey Breast   34

4.12 Oriental Lettuce-Wrapped Turkey Burgers   35

CHAPTER 5. BEEF   36

5.1 Smoky Burgers   36

5.2 Marinated Beef Ribs   36

5.3 Dark Beer-Braised Beef Ribs   36

5.4 Oriental Beef Skewers   37

5.5 Root Beer BBQ Short Ribs   37

5.6 Chili Beef Jerky   38

5.7 Reuben Sandwich — 38

5.8 Vietnamese Beef Jerky — 39

5.9 Prime Rib Roast with Mustard & Herbs — 39

5.10 Rib Eyes with Hasselback Sweet Potatoes — 39

5.11 Cajun Stuffed Peppers — 40

5.12 Smoked Meatball Rolls — 40

CHAPTER 6. CHICKEN — 42

6.1 BBQ Chicken Bacon Rolls — 42

6.2 Smoked Whole Chicken — 42

6.3 Grilled Chicken with Hot Salsa — 43

6.4 Chicken & Bacon Hot Casserole — 43

6.5 Yogurt Chicken Kebabs — 44

6.6 Grilled Thai Chicken — 44

6.7 Beer & Serrano Wings — 45

6.8 BBQ Spatchcocked Chicken — 45

6.9 Tikka Drumsticks — 46

6.10 Orange Mustard Chicken — 46

6.11 Ancho Chile BBQ Drumsticks — 47

6.12 Bacon Wrapped Chicken Skewers — 47

CHAPTER 7. PORK — 49

7.1 Prosciutto Wrapped Medjoul Dates — 49

7.2 Dried Cranberry Patties — 49

7.3 Honey Mustard Pork Loin — 50

7.4 Smoked Muffuletta Sandwich — 50

7.5 Bacon Wrapped Pork Loin — 51

7.6 Mandarin Glazed Spareribs — 51

7.7 Peaches & Bourbon Spareribs — 52

7.8 Bacon Pork Rolls — 52

7.9 Reverse-Seared Pork Chops — 52

7.10 Easy Baby Back Ribs — 53

7.11 Pulled Pork Mac & Cheese — 53

7.12 Caveman BBQ Spareribs — 54

CHAPTER 8. SEAFOOD — 55

8.1 Citrus Salmon Fillets — 55

8.2 Sake Shrimps — 55

8.3 Lemon-Herb Butter Grilled Cod — 55

8.4 Grilled Rainbow Trout — 56

8.5 Sweet & Spicy Thai Salmon — 56

8.6 Smoked Sea Bass — 57

8.7 Grilled Shrimp Cocktail — 57

8.8 Grilled Salmon with Smoked Guacamole — 58

8.9 Bacon Grilled Shrimps — 58

8.10 Simple Grilled Tuna — 59

8.11 Vodka Brined Salmon — 59

8.12 Grilled Swordfish with Salsa — 59

CHAPTER 9. DESSERTS — 61

9.1 Chocolate Brownie Cookies — 61

9.2 Gingerbread cookies — 61

9.3 Grilled Fruit with Berries & Cream — 62

9.4 Bourbon & Apple Dutch Baby — 62

9.5 Christmas Shortbread Cookies — 62

9.6 Bacon Donuts — 63

9.7 Leftover Donut Pudding — 63

9.8 Bacon Salted Caramel Brownies — 64

9.9 Blueberry Cobbler — 64

9.10 Baked Chocolate Cake — 65

9.11 Caramelized Bourbon Pears — 65

9.12 Smokey Whipped Cream — 66

INTRODUCTION

Do I Need a Wood Pellet Smoker-Grill?

The wood pellet grill not only provides the moistest foods you have ever tasted, but it's the simplest to use and sustain. Everything is controlled by software. Make sure your hopper is full of wood pellets, and your device is attached to a power source. The auger and fan are the only moving pieces in the wood pellet smoker-grill. Other smoker-grill styles have often had a tough time keeping stable temperatures due to the need to continually track the devices. For wood pellet smoker-grills, this is not required since they're built to keep temperatures consistent.

Trendy Models

Wood pellet grills merge the comfort of a barbecue grill with the taste and quality of a wood smoker, enabling you to set it and forget it. Plus, since they plug into a normal electrical socket, they do not need natural gas or propane.

From gas grills to charcoal grills, indoor grills, and beyond, it is essential to determine the right grill for you. The features of a grill such as simplicity of use and efficiency, as well as heating symmetry and cooking speed, are of utmost importance. Temperature regulation and range are critical for pellet grills. Factors such as the quality of material used, the protection it offers, the control panel, pellet dispensing mechanism, and hopper size should all be taken into account when purchasing a grill.

Considering the factors stated above, below is a list of wood pellets that are recommended. The top picks are full of features that make a perfect pellet grill, and they come from brands that are known and trusted. You will notice several sizes for any form of pellet grill and versions with unique features like functionality, Wi-Fi access, and outstanding guarantees. The safest pellet grills to purchase are as follows:

Traeger Pro Series Grill 575

D2 direct drive dynamically controls doses of pellets and airflow for optimal temperature control.

Specifications

Traeger is associated with pellet grills, and they were the first company to produce them. They're among the most common in the industry and can be used as a barbecue, smoker, or oven with precise temperature regulation. The manufactured logic sets them apart; Traeger's latest grills (including this 575 Pro) have a direct drive D2, which doses pellets and changes air flow depending on the internal setting tracked every 30 seconds by sensors.

The temperature range of the Pro 575 is 165° to 500° Fahrenheit, so it can be used for anything from barbecuing to smoking, braising, frying, and roasting. It also links to an interface with over 1,500 recipes, enabling you to program it straight from your computer and track the cooking process while doing so. You can fit as many as 16 burgers or chickens on it, plenty to feed the family and neighbors.

- Cooking surface: 572 square-inch
- Hopper capacity: 18-pound

Z Grills Wood Pellet Grill & Smoker

This Z Grills pellet grill has over 400 favorable reviews on Amazon, and this new-sounding business has been producing grills for other brands for more than 30 years. It began selling under its own label in 2017, helping it to retain its low price point. This grill has a huge cooking surface and is made of stainless steel. It has new temperature sensors that vary from 180° to 450° Fahrenheit. Although the grease collector is popular, reviewers like how simple it is to clean. It also has a complimentary grill shield.

- Cooking surface: 504 square-inch
- Hopper capacity: 20-pound

Green Mountain Davy Crockett Pellet Grill

If you are looking for a smart alternative, we suggest Green Mountain's Davy Crockett model. It has foldable legs, meaning it can take up less room in the car on game day. It is perfect for a day of tailgating or camping. It is the only compact solution with digital controls and an incorporated thermometer (called Sense-Mate) to track your beef's internal meat temperature. And, if you are too preoccupied with the game to check on your dinner, you can do it from your phone, thanks to Wi-Fi capabilities. The software also has a built-in meal timer, so you will know when it's time to feed. The cooking area is limited.

- Cooking surface: 219 square-inch
- Hopper capacity: 9-pound

Pit Boss 700FB Pellet Grill

Given its price, build quality, and capability, this is an excellent starter pellet grill. With its dial temperature monitor and quick readout show, it's a breeze to use. In addition to the multitude of grill cooking possibilities already anticipated from a pellet grill (barbecuing, grilling, and smoking), you can bake, reheat, chargrill, barbecue, and sear your food on this all-in-one device thanks to the slide-plate frame broiler. The manufacturer believes that with 700 square inches of cooking area, including the second-tier rack, you can make over 30 burgers at once.

- Cooking surface: 700 square-inch with top rack
- Hopper capacity: 21-pound

Camp Chef Woodwind Pellet Grill with Sear Box

Pellet grills have a reputation for not searing a steak as easily as a barbecue or gas grill. Camp Chef's Woodwind with Sear Box alternative can be used as a smoker, as well as a searing barbecue. For simple temperature regulation and consistent results, use the wood pellet grill, then finish with grill marks on the cast iron plate, which can hit temperatures of up to 900° Fahrenheit. Its ash-removal method makes it simpler to clean than others since ash is collected in an easy-to-remove cup beneath the smokebox. When attached, the sear box takes the role of a side rack.

- Cooking surface 429 square-inch plus 141 square-inch in the upper rack

- Hopper capacity: 24-pound

Temperature Handling

The wood pellet grill just about gains the upper hand. "Place it and forget it", says Ron Popeil of his Ronco rotisserie. As we saw earlier, the controller controls the rate of pellet flow and the fan to preserve your set-point temperature. Most manufacturers either use a third-party controller or create their own. Not every controller is the same. Some are preferable to others, and this should be considered when purchasing a wood pellet grill. Look for the controller that allows for precise temperature regulation. Analog, optical, and PID controllers are the three basic categories of controllers.

The most basic unit is an analog controller that comes with only 3 options of heating. These 3 options are low, medium, and high smoke. The bulk of these controllers are located on entry-level systems. They normally do not have a temperature probe, such as an RTD or a thermocouple, to have a feedback loop. It is the least attractive remote, and I would not purchase a machine that has one. The temperature on these systems fluctuates wildly and is unable to compensate for changes in ambient temperatures. The only power you have is the auger on and off timeframes for medium, low, and heavy, which the grill maker typically fixes.

A feedback loop is provided by a digital controller using an RTD temperature probe. A 25° Fahrenheit increment setting is standard on most digital controllers. Any digital controls may be used to replace LMH controllers with the use of an RTD temperature probe. When you hit the preset temperature, the controller runs the drill for a certain number of seconds, then turns off for a certain number of seconds and goes into idle mode before the temperature deviates a preset level, just like your home's thermostat. At that point, the loop starts again. It would help if you changed the idle mode on certain digital controls to compensate for ambient temperatures.

The most modern controllers are additive, integral, derivative (PID) controllers. They equate the target temperature to the observed temperature using a control loop input from a thermocouple temperature probe and change parameters accordingly. They encourage you to adjust the temperature of your cooking in 5-degree intervals. The PID controller controls the auger feed rate, and, in certain situations, the fan variable speeds to reduce temperature fluctuations and keep the temperature within 5° Fahrenheit of the fixed temperature, resulting in highly precise temperature regulation. PID-type controllers are standard on most high-end wood pellet grills, and they use optimization algorithms fine-tuned for the units.

Various controllers, such as the digital control panel of Pellet Boss (MAK Grills), have 1 or more meat temperature probes and custom programming elements to improve your cooking experience while giving you complete control over any element of your cook.

Choose a wood pellet grill with a digital controller at the very least, and ideally one with a PID-based controller.

Smoking

What it is:

Smoking is the method of using smoke and low, indirect heat to cook and preserve foods, particularly meat. It has been used to prevent food from spoiling since the time of the savages. Refrigerators are now used less for storage and more for imparting smoky taste and tenderness to poultry, foods, and fish by cooking them at low temperatures for prolonged periods.

It is all focused on science. Flaming breaks down the collagen in meat, resulting in tenderness that melts in your mouth. To get the best performance, season the meat with a dry rub or brine before smoking it.

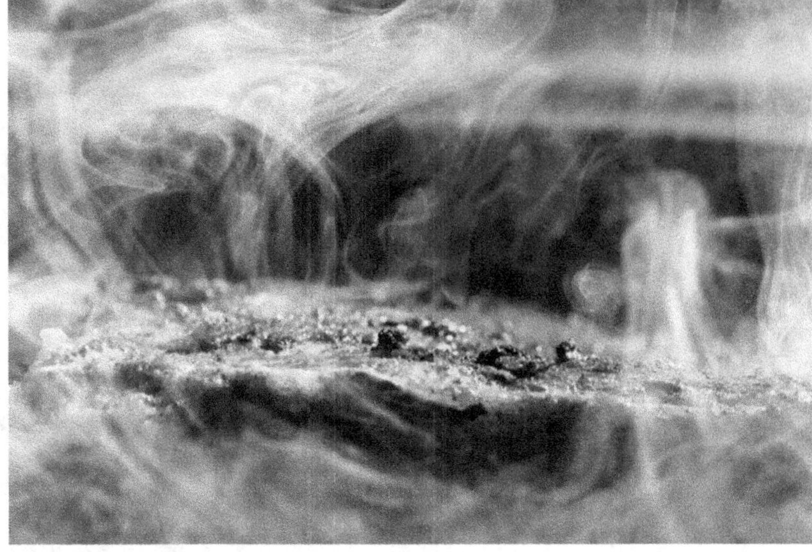

Equipment:

Metal chambers heated with steam, charcoal, or wood chips generate low and steady heat (between 200° and 250° Fahrenheit) and a tone of smoke in advanced meat smokers. If you go for wood, each form of wood has a distinct taste, and there are many to choose from. Though gas and charcoal grills may be adapted to smoke meats, smokers designed exclusively for smoking are the simplest for beginners to use.

Characteristics:

A smoke ring, a pink-tinged coating of meat just under the meat's crust or "bark," can be seen on nearly all smoked meats. It happens because nitrogen dioxide in smoke stops myoglobin from browning the beef. It is a hallmark of steady-smoked beef, but many scientists say it could be manipulated with sodium nitrite or curing salt (pink).

Recipes to try:

For your next Thanksgiving meal, consider traditional smoked ribs and brisket, or branch out to smoked chicken and trout.

Grilling

What it is:

Grilling meat means exposing it to high glowing heat, usually done on grates set over a heat source like charcoal or wood. Making a caramelized crust on the exterior of the grilled beef helps to seal in moisture and cook the inside. Fun fact: backyard grilling as we know it originated after World War II, as the middle class migrated to the suburbs.

Equipment:

Grills are available in various forms, shapes, sizes, and heat sources, ranging from charcoal to petrol. Charcoal grills provide a smokier taste, which is perfect for flavorful steaks and burgers. Gas grills fueled by propane are more popular and can cook anything from veggies to hot dogs.

"An immediate read thermometer is your best option for ensuring the meat and fish are grilled to the correct temperature," says grill master Bobby Flay of other equipment. Tongs are often good for transferring food from the grill to the plate, and there are several fancy devices to use if you are feeling adventurous.

Characteristics:

Since it uses direct heat to cook the meats or other ingredients, grilling is a far quicker option than smoking. It leaves a crusty, blackened char on the outside of the beef, which tests suggest may be harmful if consumed in large quantities. A grill is more flexible than smoking in that it can cook pizza, veggies, and even fruit.

Recipes to try:

At your next cookout, consider pizza, burgers, or salmon, and for the vegetarians, try any of those meat-free recipes that cook well on a barbecue.

Grilling vs Smoking: Which One to Choose?

The most significant difference between smoking and grilling is the amount of time needed. Smoking will take all day and needs regular temperature control to ensure that the meat cooks uniformly. While grilling is more convenient and faster, smoking produces a tender and tasty product that is almost impossible to duplicate.

Slighter meats like chicken and steak cook best on a grill, whereas larger meats like ribs and briskets profit from big smokers. You will serve tasty food to friends and relatives at this summer's barbecues, regardless of the tool you choose. Grilling is about rapidly cooking food over a high heat source (fueled by gas or charcoal). In the case of grilling, hot and quick means cooking at 350° Fahrenheit or higher in less than one hour. While smoking is just like a more intense form of barbecuing: you are cooking the meat with smoke through roiling chunks or pieces of hickory, apple, mesquite, or cherry, which imparts its own taste to the meat.

Smoking takes place at a lower temperature than grilling to ensure that the smoky taste pervades the meat while still cooking it thoroughly. To smoke food, your grill should be set around 125° to 175°

Fahrenheit; any hotter, and the exterior sections of the food will cook very quickly, creating a barrier that the smoke cannot pass through. But the grilling temperatures should be about 450° to 500° Fahrenheit for things like chops and steaks to enable for quick cooking times. Remember that the tenderest pieces, such as strip steaks, ribeye steaks, rib and small loin primal pieces and T-bones are the best for grilling. A great way to maintain the tenderness and avoid drying out and overcooking is to cook them quickly. Cooking a juicy, tasty slice of meat over a hot flame for a brief period is the perfect way to do it.

1.1 Spicy & Smoky Cashews

Preparation time: 5 minutes

Cooking time: 1 hour

Servings: 6

Ingredients

- One tbsp chili paste
- One tbsp simple syrup
- Zest of one lemon
- A half tbsp chopped rosemary
- One tsp hot pepper flakes
- One pinch cayenne powder
- One lb. cashews

Steps

- Set grill temperature to 220° F, then keep the lid closed for fifteen minutes.
- Combine the syrup, chili paste, rosemary, lemon zest, cayenne & red pepper flakes in a small bowl. Pour the mixture over the cashews & thoroughly mix to coat.
- On a sheet tray spread the cashews. Put them straight on the grill grate. Cook the nuts for around one hour, stirring sometimes.
- Take the cashews from the grill, allow to cool & serve.
-

1.2. Asian Jumbo Shrimps

Preparation time: 2 hours

Cooking time: 5 minutes

Servings: 4

Ingredients

- Four lbs. jumbo shrimps
- One cup soy sauce
- One cup teriyaki sauce
- One cup white vermouth
- One cup olive oil
- One clove garlic, chopped
- One tsp fresh ginger, grated
- One tsp chicken rub

Steps

- Cut the shrimp heads, shell them & remove the & black veins.
- In a small bowl combine all the other ingredients; add the shrimps & mix thoroughly. Put the shrimp in the refrigerator & let marinate for 2-4 hours.
- Set grill temperature to 450°F, then keep the lid closed for fifteen minutes.
- Drain the shrimp from the marinade & thread them onto pre-soaked wooden skewers.
- Put the shrimp skewers on the grill grate, close the lid, & cook for around three minutes.
- Flip the shrimp skewers, close the lid & cook for an extra three minutes.
- Take the skewers from the grill & serve.

1.3 Shrimp Stuffed Jalapeños

Preparation time: 10 minutes

Cooking time: 55 minutes

Servings: 6

Ingredients

- Eight shrimp shelled & deveined
- Half tsp chicken rub
- One tbsp olive oil
- Six jalapeño peppers
- Eight oz cream cheese
- Two tbsp chopped coriander
- Half cup dry coconut flakes
- Twelve slices smoked bacon

Steps

- Set grill temperature to 420°F, then keep the lid closed for fifteen minutes.
- Season the shrimps with the olive oil & chicken rub.
- Put the shrimps on the grill grate & cook them for around five minutes each side.
- Remove the shrimp & allow to cool.
- Lower the temp of the grill to 320°F.
- Cut the peppers in half & remove the seeds.
- In a blender, mince the shrimp together with the softened cream cheese, & coriander.
- Fill each pepper half with the mixture & sprinkle coconut flakes on top.
- Wrap every stuffed half pepper with a bacon slice & put them on a baking sheet, lined with foil.
- Cook the peppers for around 45 minutes or until the bacon gets golden & crispy. Serve.

1.4 Garlic Mozzarella Bread

Preparation time: 10 minutes

Cooking time: 20 minutes

Servings: 4

Ingredients

- One baguette or bread loaf
- Half cup butter, softened
- Half cup mayonnaise
- One tbsp dried oregano
- Four garlic cloves, minced
- One tbsp red pepper flakes
- One pinch salt
- One cup mozzarella cheese, diced

Steps

- Set grill temperature to 350°F, then keep the lid closed for fifteen minutes.
- Slice the bread loaf in half lengthwise.
- In a small bowl combine the mayonnaise, butter, garlic, salt, pepper flakes & oregano. Mix thoroughly.
- Spread the butter mixture on the loaf halves & top it with parmesan & mozzarella cheese.
- Put the bread on the grill grate. Grill for around 20 minutes. Serve hot.

1.5 Tennessee Whiskey Bacon

Preparation time: 10 minutes

Cooking time: 20 minutes

Servings: 4

Ingredients

- One lb. smoked bacon, sliced
- One cup Tennessee or Bourbon Whiskey
- One cup apple juice
- One tbsp chicken rub
- Half cup white flour
- Half cup brown sugar
- One tsp ground black pepper

Steps

- Put the bacon slices into a big resealable bag.
- Pour in a bowl the whisky & apple juice; add the chicken rub & whisk thoroughly. Add the seasoned liquid to the bacon & seal the bag.

- Let the bacon marinate in the fridge for around half an hour.
- In another resealable bag, add the brown sugar, black pepper & flour; shake well to mix.
- Drain the bacon slices from the marinade & put them in the flour mixture bag; shake well to coat evenly. Then proceed with the net bacon slice.
- Arrange the bacon slices on a baking pan in a single layer.
- Set grill temperature to 350°F, then keep the lid closed for fifteen minutes.
- Bake the bacon slices until golden brown & crisp, around 20 minutes. Serve.

1.6 Spiced Jalapeño Balls

Preparation time: 15 minutes

Cooking time: 45 minutes

Servings: 8

Ingredients

- Four oz cream cheese
- Half cup cheddar cheese, shredded
- One tbsp coriander, minced
- Six Jalapeño peppers
- Two lbs. ground pork
- Two tbsp chicken rub

Steps

- Set grill temperature to 350°F, then keep the lid closed for fifteen minutes.
- Combine cheddar, coriander & cream cheese in a bowl & mix thoroughly.
- Divide in half lengthwise & seed the peppers; spoon the cheese mix in each half. Divide again in half each stuffed half pepper.
- Take a small handful of ground meat, flatten it, put a piece of pepper on it & wrap the meat around to make a meatball; shape it well in your hands. Repeat for each piece.
- Season each meatball with the pork rub.
- On the grill grate, put the balls straight & cook for around thirty minutes, till browned & cooked through, flipping them at least once. Serve.

1.7 Wild Boar Sausage

Preparation time: 1o minutes

Cooking time: 4 hours

Servings: 4

Ingredients

- One lb. Ground Wild Boar
- One tsp Kosher Salt
- Half tsp sugar
- One tsp pork rub
- One tbsp yellow mustard
- Half tsp black pepper
- Half tsp onion powder

Steps

- In a bowl, combine all ingredients, being careful not to overmix. Cover with cling film & refrigerate for the night.
- Shape the meat into a loaf, roll it in a cling film sheet & twist the ends to give it a regular shape. Unwrap slowly
- Set grill temperature to 350°F, then keep the lid closed for fifteen minutes.
- Place the loaf directly onto the grill grate & cook for around three to four hours. When cooked, let the loaf cool for one hour at room temp.
- Slice & serve.

1.8 Southern Stuffed Peppers

Preparation time: 15 minutes

Cooking time: 40 minutes

Servings: 6

Ingredients

- Six large red bell peppers
- One pound ground pork
- One onion, chopped
- Two garlic cloves, chopped
- Two tbsp pork rub
- Half cup tomato sauce
- Two cups cooked rice

- One cup cooked black beans, drained
- One cup fresh corn
- Half cup cheddar cheese, grated

Steps

- Wash & dry the peppers; slice them in half & remove the seeds.
- To prepare the stuffing, in a big frying pan, brown the ground pork, breaking any lump with a wooden spatula.
- When browned, add garlic & onion & stir fry for three more minutes. Add the tomato sauce, pork rub, black beans, corn & rice; cook till the flavors are mixed, around five minutes. Let it cool.
- Fill every pepper half with the prepared stuffing, taking care not to overmix.
- Set the grill temp to 350°F, then keep the lid closed for 15 minutes.
- Arrange the peppers, filling side up, directly on the hot grill grate. Cook for around 35 minutes.
- When cooked, sprinkle the grated cheese on the peppers; close the grill lid & cook for five more minutes, to melt the cheese. Serve.

1.9 Grilled Chicken Legs with Spicy Salsa

Preparation time: 15 minutes

Cooking time: 40 minutes

Servings: 6

Ingredients

For the chicken

- Six whole chicken legs
- Two tbsp olive oil
- One tbsp smoked paprika
- One tsp ground coriander
- One tsp ground turmeric
- Zest of one lime
- Half tsp kosher salt
- One tsp ground black pepper

For the salsa

- Four jalapeño peppers
- Four garlic cloves, chopped
- Six sprigs fresh coriander
- Two spring onions, chopped
- One tbsp lime juice
- Two tbsp maple syrup
- Half cup white wine vinegar
- One tsp kosher salt

Steps

- In a big bowl combine the chicken, smoked paprika, olive oil, lime zest, coriander, pepper & salt, mixing well to season. Cover it with cling film & put it in the refrigerator for 4 hours or overnight.
- Set the grill temp to 350°F, then keep the lid closed for 15 minutes.
- Put the chicken thighs directly on the hot on the grill grates, skin side down.
- Cook until perfectly grilled, around 40-45 minutes.
- In the meanwhile, prepare the hot salsa. Put the peppers on the hot grill grates, beside the chicken & cook for around 25-30 minutes. Remove the peppers from the grill, let them cool a bit & remove seeds & stems Blend in a mixer the jalapeños with all the other salsa ingredient, pulsing until smooth.
- Serve the chicken with the spicy jalapeño salsa.

1.10 Bacon & Cheddar Baby Potatoes

Preparation time: 30 minutes

Cooking time: 40 minutes

Servings: 6

Ingredients

- Two lbs. baby potatoes
- One quarter cup olive oil
- One tsp garlic powder
- One tsp onion powder
- One tbsp smoked paprika
- One tbsp dried chives
- Two cups cheddar cheese, shredded
- One lb. cooked bacon, crumbled
- One bunch spring onions, chopped
- 4 tbsp sour cream

Steps

- Boil/microwave the baby potatoes till fork tender, then let them cool at room temp.
- Mix the garlic powder, olive oil, paprika, chives & onion powder in a large bowl. Pour in the potatoes & toss to coat well in the seasoning. Place the potatoes on a paper-lined cookie tray; with a fork, lightly smash every potato to flatten.
- Set the grill temp to 450°F, then keep the lid closed for 15 minutes.
- Grill the potatoes for around twenty to thirty minutes till their color changes to golden & crispy, flipping them once. When cooked, sprinkle the potatoes with the bacon, spring onions & cheddar. Close the lid & grill for ten minutes more to let the cheese melt.
- Take the potatoes from the grill & season with the sour cream. Serve.

1.11 Spicy Nachos Dip

Preparation time: 15 minutes

Cooking time: 40 minutes

Servings: 6

Ingredients

- Two tbsp olive oil
- One red onion, diced
- One & half tsp kosher salt
- Two lbs. ground beef
- Two tbsp beef rub
- Two cups roasted tomatoes with their juices
- Two cups cooked black beans, drained
- Half cup green chiles, diced
- One bunch spring onions, chopped
- Half cup white rice, uncooked

Steps

- Set the grill temp to 400°F, place a 12-inch cast-iron skillet on the grill, then keep the lid closed for 15 minutes to preheat.
- Once the grill temp is set, put the onions, oil & half tsp salt into the skillet. Close the lid & cook, stirring once or twice, till the onions are tender, around ten minutes.
- Add the meat & one tsp salt 1 tsp, then cook for about 15-20 minutes till browned, breaking any lump with a wooden spatula. Add the beef rub & mix.
- Add the beans, tomatoes, green chiles, rice, & one cup of water. Mix well to ensure the liquid is covering the rice.

- Cover the skillet with a lid, close the grill lid & cook for twenty to twenty-five minutes or till the rice is completely cooked & all the liquid has been absorbed.
- Remove the skillet lid & sprinkle the cheese on top; close the grill lid again, till the cheese melts.
- Remove the dip from the grill, sprinkle with the green onions & serve with corn chips.

1.12 Red Onion Jam, Duck Confit & Goat Cheese Croutons

Preparation time: 5 minutes

Cooking time: 45 minutes

Servings: 6

Ingredients

- Two tbsp butter
- Three red onions, sliced
- Two garlic cloves, shopped
- 4 tbsp sugar
- Pepper
- 4 tbsp dry red wine
- One tbsp apple cider vinegar
- Zest of one lemon
- Four prepared confit duck legs
- One baguette, sliced
- Half cup herbed goat cheese, crushed
- Olive oil
- 4 tbsp pomegranate arils
- Sea salt
- Black pepper, crushed

Steps

- Set the grill temp to 350°F, then keep the lid closed for 15 minutes.
- In a pan over low heat melt the butter; add the garlic, onions & sugar, then season with sea salt. Cover & cook till softened & caramelized, around 20-30 minutes. Take it from the heat & whisk in the vinegar, lemon zest & red wine. Set aside.
- Line a cookie tray with bakery paper. Place the duck legs on the tray, skin side, & put the tray on the grill grate. Cook for around eight to ten minutes, till the skin begins to crisp & the meat breaks easily with the fork. Remove from the grill & chop the meat with two forks.
- In the meantime, drizzle every baguette slice with olive oil & season with salt & pepper. Put the slices on the hot grill grate & cook till the grill marks develop, & the bread gets golden.
- Build the crostini putting on the grilled bread slices the red onion jam, pulled duck, goat cheese & pomegranate. Serve.

2.1 Mashed Smoky Potatoes

Preparation time: 5 minutes

Cooking time: 45 minutes

Servings: 6

Ingredients

- Half cup heavy cream, whipped
- Five lbs. potatoes
- Half stick butter, softened
- White pepper
- Kosher salt

Steps

- Set the grill temp to 300°F, then keep the lid closed for 15 minutes.
- Peel the potatoes & cut them into half-inch cubes. Place the cubes in a baking dish, add half cup of water & place the dish on the grill grate. Close the lid & cook for around 40 minutes, or until the potatoes are fork tender.
- Mix butter & cream in a medium saucepan. Melt the butter mix over medium heat.
- Remove the potatoes from the grill & drain the water.
- Mash the potatoes in a dish, then gradually add the butter & cream mixture, mixing with a spatula, taking cate not to overmix. Season with pepper & salt to taste & serve

2.2 Caesar Salad on the Grill

Preparation time: 5 minutes

Cooking time: 5 minutes

Servings: 4

Ingredients

- One cup mayonnaise
- Two cloves garlic
- One tsp French mustard
- Four tbsp Parmesan cheese, grated
- Black pepper
- One tsp Worcestershire sauce
- One pinch salt
- Six tbsp olive oil
- Two heads romaine lettuce
- Crostini for serving

Steps

- For the dressing, add the garlic, mayonnaise, French mustard, Worcestershire sauce, Parmesan cheese, pepper & salt in a blender or food processor, then gradually pour four tbsp olive oil till smooth. Keep refrigerated.
- Cut the Romaine lettuce it in half longitudinally, leaving the edges unbroken to prevent the leaves to fall apart. Rinse & dry the lettuce halves.
- Set the grill temp to 500°F, then keep the lid closed for 15 minutes.
- Brush the halves of Romaine with the leftover two tbsp olive oil & place them cut edge down on the grill until light grill marks appear.
- Remove the lettuce from the grill, top with the dressing & serve with crostini.

2.3. Smoked Mediterranean Potato Salad

Preparation time: 10 minutes

Cooking time: 45 minutes

Servings: 4

- One tbsp salt
- Two tbsp olive oil
- Half tsp black pepper
- Two lbs. small potatoes
- Sea Salt
- Two cups mayonnaise
- Four tbsp Sriracha hot sauce
- One tbsp basil, chopped
- One tbsp chives, chopped
- One tbsp parsley, chopped

Steps

- Set the grill temp to 250°F, then keep the lid closed for 15 minutes.
- Place the potatoes on a cookie sheet, season with pepper & salt & toss with olive oil. Place the cookie sheet on the grill grate & smoke for around 15-20 minutes.
- Take the potatoes from the grill, raise the temp to 500°F, then keep the lid closed for 15 minutes.
- Put the potatoes back on the grill for another 20 to 25 minutes, or till fork tender. Let them cool.
- While the potatoes are cooking, combine in a bowl the Sriracha sauce & mayonnaise. Add the potatoes, parsley, chives & basil. Serve.

2.4 Potato & Scallion Salad

Preparation time: 15 minutes

Cooking time: 15 minutes

Servings: 6

Ingredients

- Ten scallions, whole
- Half lb. small potatoes, cooked & halved
- Black pepper to taste
- 6 tbsp olive oil
- Two tsp Kosher salt
- Two tsp lemon juice
- Two tbsp rice vinegar
- One small jalapeño, Sliced

Steps

- Set the grill temp to 450°F, then keep the lid closed for 15 minutes.
- Brush the scallions with two tbsp olive oil & place them directly on the hot grill grate.
- Cook for two to three minutes, or until slightly charred. Remove from heat & allow it to cool.
- Cut the scallions & set them aside until they have cooled.
- In a bowl season the potatoes with pepper to taste, one tbsp salt & drizzle with two tbsp olive oil. Place the potatoes on the hot grill grates for 4 to 5 minutes, or until grilled thoroughly.
- In a mixing bowl, whisk together the remaining two tbsp olive oil, one teaspoon salt, lemon juice, & rice vinegar. Add the scallions, potatoes, & jalapeno slices. Mix & serve.

2.5 Skillet Roasted Vegetables

Preparation time: 10 minutes

Cooking time: 25 minutes

Servings: 4

Ingredients

- One half head yellow cauliflower, divided into florets
- One half head purple cauliflower, divided into florets
- Four cups butternut squash, cubed
- Three tbsp olive oil
- Two cups Shiitake or Oyster mushrooms, chopped

- Black pepper to taste
- Two tsp Kosher Salt
- 4 tbsp parsley, chopped

- Set the grill temp to 450°F, then keep the lid closed for 15 minutes.
- Add all the vegetables to a big mixing bowl. Sprinkle the olive oil on top, then season with salt & pepper tossing to coat properly.
- Place the vegetables on cookie sheet, taking care not to overcrowd them.
- Cook for about 15 minutes, then stir & cook for another five to fifteen minutes, or until the veggies' edges are nicely browned.
- Take the vegetables from the grill, garnish with parsley & serve right away, or let them cool at room temperature.

2.6 Grilled Bacon & Green Beans

Preparation time: 5 minutes

Cooking time: 20 minutes

Servings: 4

Ingredients

- Half lb. green beans, ends trimmed
- Four strips bacon, sliced
- Four tbsp olive oil
- Two garlic cloves, crushed
- One tsp kosher salt

Steps

- Set the grill temp to 350°F, then keep the lid closed for 15 minutes.
- Combine all ingredients in a mixing bowl & spread uniformly on a cookie sheet.
- Put the tray straight on the grill & cook for around 20 minutes, or till the bacon is crunchy & the beans are slightly browned. Serve.

2.7 Garlic Herbed Potato Wedges

Preparation time: 10 minutes

Cooking time: 45 minutes

Servings: 6

Ingredients

- Six large potatoes, sliced into wedges
- Three tbsp olive oil
- Six cloves garlic, crushed
- One tbsp fresh thyme, chopped
- One tbsp fresh rosemary, chopped
- Black pepper to taste
- Sea salt

Steps

- Set the grill temp to 350°F, then keep the lid closed for 15 minutes.
- Line a big baking sheet with parchment paper. Place the potatoes in a big bowl, drizzle with olive oil & add the thyme, garlic, rosemary, season with pepper & salt. Toss all together to combine.
- Arrange the potato wedge on the baking sheet, place it on the grill grates, close the lid & cook for 40 to 45 minutes or till potatoes are golden brown & cooked through. Serve.

2.8 Grilled Cabbage with Bacon Mustard Vinaigrette

Preparation time: 10 minutes

Cooking time: 10 minutes

Servings: 4

Ingredients

- Three strips bacon, sliced
- Two tbsp sherry vinegar
- One shallot, minced
- One tbsp French mustard
- One head green cabbage
- Four tbsp olive oil
- One tsp fresh thyme, chopped
- Pepper & salt

Steps

- Set the grill temp to 450°F, then keep the lid closed for 15 minutes.
- Prepare the vinaigrette: brown the bacon in two tbsp olive oil in a skillet over medium heat till crisp. Take the skillet from the heat, add the vinegar, shallot, thyme & mustard, mix well & set aside.
- Cut the cabbage lengthwise in 6 slices, drizzle with the leftover olive oil & season with pepper & salt. Grill the cabbage steaks straight on the grill grate for 5 minutes on each side.
- Take the cabbage steaks from the grill, arrange on a serving platter & top with the bacon vinaigrette. Serve.

2.9 Grilled Beet Salad with Bacon

Preparation time: 15 minutes

Cooking time: 45 minutes

Servings: 4

Ingredients

- Four tbsp prepared vinaigrette,
- Two raw beets, peeled & sliced
- Two pears, sliced
- Two avocados, diced
- One red leaf lettuce head, cut into pieces
- Eight strips bacon, sliced
- Four tbsp pecans

Steps

- Set the grill temp to 450°F, then keep the lid closed for 15 minutes.
- Spread the beet slices on a parchment-lined cookie sheet, with bacon on top. Cook for 25 minutes.
- Stir the beet slices in the bacon fat to coat them & gook for additional 15 minutes or till the beets are soft & the bacon is crispy
- Toss in the pecans & cook for additional 5 minutes. Remove the sheet from the grill & let cool a bit.
- In a big salad bowl, combine the beets, bacon, pecans, avocado, pears, & lettuce. Add the vinaigrette, toss to mix & serve.

2.10 Grilled Lettuce Salad

Preparation time: 10 minutes

Cooking time: 10 minutes

Servings: 2

Ingredients

Dressing

- One cup mayonnaise
- Four oz blue cheese
- Four tbsp buttermilk
- One clove garlic, minced
- Pepper & salt
- Two tbsp parsley, chopped
- Two strips bacon
- One tbsp olive oil

Main

- One head romaine lettuce, halved
- Two tomatoes, chopped

- Eight oz blue cheese, crumbled
- One scallion, chopped

Steps

- In a small sized bowl, whisk together all the dressing ingredients & set aside.
- Set the grill temp to 400°F, then keep the lid closed for 15 minutes.
- Place the bacon strips straight on the grill grate & cook for around 10 minutes, or till the bacon is crispy & the fat has been rendered. Take from the grill & crumble.
- Drizzle olive oil over romaine lettuce & season with pepper & salt. Put the wedges on the grill grate & cook for around 6 minutes cut side down, till slightly browned & grill marks appear.
- Take the romaine from the grill, place on a serving dish & drizzle with the seasoning. Add on top the tomatoes, parsley, crumbled bacon, scallions & blue cheese. Serve.

2.11 Spiced Carrot Salad with Pomegranate Relish

Preparation time: 10 minutes

Cooking time: 30 minutes

Servings: 6

Ingredients

Main

- One tsp coriander
- Two tbsp olive oil
- Half tsp cumin
- Two bunches carrots
- Two tsp salt
- Two garlic cloves, minced
- Zest of one lime
- Two tsp fennel seeds
- One tsp sugar

Relish

- Four tbsp fresh mint, chopped
- Half cup cashews, chopped
- One tbsp fresh thyme

- Salt
- Four tbsp parsley, chopped
- Three tbsp olive oil
- Half cup pomegranate seeds
- Juice of one lime

Steps

- Set the grill temp to 400°F, then keep the lid closed for 15 minutes.
- Wash thoroughly the carrots but leave the skins on. Place the sugar, spices & salt in a big bowl, add the carrots, garlic, olive oil & toss to coat well.
- Arrange the carrots on a cookie sheet & cook for 30 minutes in the grill, stirring once. When the carrots are fork tender, remove them. Lastly, grate the lime zest on top.
- Meanwhile prepare the relish: mix in a bowl the olive oil, cashews, pomegranate seeds, lime juice, herbs & a pinch of salt. Taste for salt.
- Arrange the carrots on a serving & top with the pomegranate & cashew relish. Serve.

2.12 Vermouth Grilled Root Vegetables

Preparation time: 20 minutes

Cooking time: 1 hour

Servings: 8

Ingredients

- One red onion, cut into wedges
- Two turnips, peeled & cut into wedges
- One fennel bulb, cut into wedges
- Three tbsp olive oil
- Four tbsp dry vermouth
- Eight small potatoes, cut into wedges
- One head garlic
- Two tsp veggie rub
- Two golden beets, cut into wedges
- Two cups carrots, cut into one-inch pieces
- Two parsnips, cut into one-inch pieces

- On a big sheet tray, spread out the wedged vegetables.
- Cut the top of the garlic head to reveal the clove tops. Put the garlic on an aluminum foil square, drizzle with one tablespoon olive oil & loosely wrap the foil around the garlic. Add the garlic to vegetables on the tray.
- Drizzle the rest of the olive oil on the vegetables. Add the dry vermouth, veggie rub & thyme in a mixing bowl. Stir the vegetables to combine.
- Set the grill temp to 500°F, then keep the lid closed for 15 minutes.
- Cook the vegetables for 60 to 90 minutes till tender & starting to brown.
- Unpack the garlic cloves & squeeze them on the vegetables, stirring to mix. Serve.

CHAPTER 3. LAMB

3.1 Roasted Lamb Leg

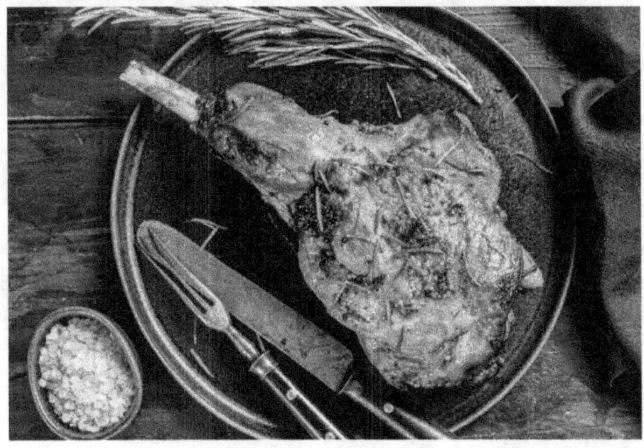

Preparation time: 30 minutes

Cooking time: 1 hour

Servings: 8

Ingredients

- One leg of lamb, around 8 lbs.
- Four garlic cloves, sliced
- One tbsp garlic, minced
- Four sprigs rosemary
- Two tsp olive oil
- Two lemons
- Black pepper, to taste
- Salt, to taste

Steps

- Combine the minced garlic & olive oil in a mixing bowl. Rub the lamb leg with the mixture.
- Make around two dozen thin, deep perforations in the lamb leg using a paring knife. Fill the holes with slices of garlic & rosemary sprigs.
- Juice & zest the lemons, then uniformly distribute the zest & juice above the lamb. Season the lamb with pepper & salt.

- Set the grill temp to 500°F, then keep the lid closed for 15 minutes. Place the lamb directly on the grill grates & cook for thirty minutes.
- Lower the grill temperature to 350°f & cook for 60 to 90 minutes, or till the internal temperature ranges 130°f for medium-rare. Allow 15 minutes for the lamb to rest before carving

3.2 Braised Lamb Shank

Preparation time: 15 minutes

Cooking time: 4 hours

Servings: 4

Ingredients

- Four lamb shanks, whole
- One cup red wine
- Four sprigs rosemary
- Four sprigs thyme
- Pork rub, to taste
- One cup beef stock

Steps

- Sprinkle the lamb shanks with pork rub to taste.
- Set the grill temp to 500°F, then keep the lid closed for 15 minutes.
- Cook the shanks straight on the grill grate for 20 minutes or till the outside is browned.
- Transfer the shanks to a dutch oven. Pour the beef broth & red wine over the shanks, add the herbs & close the lid. Reduce the grill temperature to 325°F & place the dutch oven on the grill grate.
- Cook the shanks for at least 3 to 4 hours or till they reach an internal temperature of 180°F.

- Remove the dutch oven from the grill, transfer the shanks with their juice to a serving platter & serve.

3.3 Lamb Kebabs

Preparation time: 15 minutes

Cooking time: 10 minutes

Servings: 4

Ingredients

- Half cup olive oil
- Three lbs. boneless lamb, cut into one-inch cubes
- One tsp cumin
- Two tbsp cilantro, chopped
- Zest of one lemon
- Two red onions, Cut into squares
- Two tsp black pepper
- Two tbsp mint, chopped
- Salt, to taste
- Half cup lemon juice
- Fifteen dried apricots, halved

Steps

- In a medium mixing bowl, whisk together the olive oil, pepper, salt, zest, lemon juice, cumin, cilantro, & mint. Add the lamb shoulder & toss to properly coat. Refrigerate for at least one night to marinate.
- Remove the lamb from the marinade & thread on skewers, alternating meat, apricots & red onion till the skewer is full.
- Set the grill temp to 400°F, then keep the lid closed for 15 minutes.
- Place the skewers straight on the grill grate & cook for 8-10 minutes or more, if you like the meat well done.
- Remove the skewers & serve with your favorite sides, such as couscous, rice or pita bread.

3.4 BBQ Lamb Pocket with Tzatziki

Preparation time: 1 hour

Cooking time: 2 hours

Servings: 4

Ingredients

- One leg of lamb
- Two lemons, juiced
- Two tbsp olive oil
- Two cups greek yogurt
- Three tomatoes, diced
- Black pepper, to taste
- Two cucumbers, grated
- Zest of two lemons
- Two tbsp mint leaves
- Salt, to taste
- Twelve pita breads
- Four tbsp dill, chopped
- One red onion, thinly sliced
- Eight oz feta cheese, crumbled
- Two garlic cloves, grated
- Chicken rub, to taste

Steps

- Remove the lamb from the fridge & set it aside to let it come to room temperature.
- Rub the lemon juice & olive oil all over the lamb. Season with chicken rub & let rest.

- Set the grill temp to 450°F, then keep the lid closed for 15 minutes.
- Cook the lamb for at least 30 minutes, then lower the heat to 350°F & cook until the thickest part of meat's internal temperature reaches 140°F for medium-rare or more, if desired.
- Prepare the tzatziki sauce. In a bowl mix the yogurt, garlic, cucumbers, mint, dill, lemon juice & zest, salt & pepper to taste. Place in the refrigerator to chill.
- When the meat is almost ready, cover the pitas in aluminum foil & put on the grill grate to warm.
- Place the cooked lamb on a cutting board, let rest for 15 minutes & slice the meat.
- Cut each pita bread in half, lengthwise, to obtain two pockets. Fill the pita pockets with the lamb, feta crumbles, tzatziki sauce, red onion & diced tomato.
- Serve the pockets with fries.

3.5 Smoked Lamb Sausage

Preparation time: 2 hours

Cooking time: 1 hour

Servings: 6

Ingredients

- Two lbs. boned lamb shoulder
- One tbsp garlic, minced
- One tsp cumin
- One tsp smoked paprika
- Two tbsp fennel, ground
- One hog casing
- One tbsp cilantro, chopped
- Half tsp cayenne pepper
- One tbsp parsley, chopped
- One tsp black pepper
- One garlic clove
- Two tbsp salt

Yogurt sauce

- Three cups greek yogurt
- Juice of one lemon
- One garlic clove
- One cucumber, peeled
- One tbsp dill, chopped
- Salt, to taste
- Pepper, to taste

Steps

- Cut the lamb meat into chunks & grind in a meat grinder.
- In a bowl, mix the ground lamb with all the spices & herbs. Keep refrigerated so that the fat does not melt.
- Attach a sausage horn to the meat grinder. Attach the hog casing to the horn & start feeding the sausage. As the sausage is forming, twist it into links.
- Stab holes all along the sausage with help a paring knife to allow steam to get out while cooking. Keep the sausage refrigerated until ready to cook.
- Prepare the yogurt sauce in a medium-sized mixing bowl, mixing all the ingredients. Cover & store in the refrigerator.
- Set the grill temp to 225°F, then keep the lid closed for 15 minutes.
- Place the sausage directly on the grill grate & smoke the sausage for 1 hour.
- Remove the sausage from the grill, cut into links & the grill temperature to 500°F.
- Put the sausage links back onto the grill grate & cook for five minutes on either side.
- Serve immediately with the yogurt sauce.

3.6 Special Grilled Lamb Burgers

Preparation time: 20 minutes

Cooking time: 30 minutes

Servings: 4

- Two lbs. lamb, ground
- Eight slices cheddar cheese
- Two tbsp mint, chopped
- Two tbsp dill, chopped
- One jalapeño pepper, chopped
- One cup mayonnaise
- Five garlic cloves,
- One red bell pepper
- Pepper & salt, to taste
- Two tsp lemon juice
- Six scallions, minced
- Four hamburger buns
- One cup rocket
- One red onion, sliced
- One tomato, thinly sliced

Steps

- Set the grill temp to 450°F, then keep the lid closed for 15 minutes.
- In a mixing bowl combine the ground lamb, 3 minced garlic cloves, jalapeno, scallions, mint, & dill. Season with salt & mix thoroughly to combine.
- Shape the lamb mixture into eight patties & set aside.
- Put the red bell pepper directly on the grill grate & cook for twenty minutes, turning it a quarter turn on every 5 minutes or till charred all over.
- Take the pepper off the grill & put it into a big zip-top bag. After 10 minutes take the from the bag, cut in half, remove the seeds & peel off the skin.
- In a food processor, combine the roasted red pepper, 2 garlic cloves, mayonnaise, lemon juice, pepper & salt to taste. Process till smooth. Set it aside.
- Cook the lamb burgers for 5 minutes on each side for medium doneness or till desired. Put the buns on the grill grate, cut side down, to toast for the last few minutes of cooking & top the burgers with a cheese slice.
- Spread the pepper mayo on the toasted buns, arrange two burgers on top, & garnish with arugula, tomato & onion. Serve with a side dish of your choice.

3.7 Pulled Lamb Shoulder

Preparation time: 2 hours

Cooking time: 5 hours

Servings: 4

Ingredients

- One tsp cumin seeds
- One tbsp lime juice
- Three lbs. lamb shoulder
- One tsp pumpkin seeds
- One tbsp smoked paprika
- Three cloves garlic
- Two tbsp olive oil
- Two oz guajillo peppers, seeded
- One tbsp salt
- One tbsp fresh oregano
- One tsp coriander seeds

Steps

- Finely grind the cumin, pumpkin & coriander seeds in a spice grinder.
- Place the cover guajillo chilies in a microwave-safe bowl, cover with water & microwave on high for around 2 minutes. Cool slightly & transfer to a food processor bowl along with 2 tbsp of water.
- Add the paprika, oregano, ground seeds, olive oil, lime juice, garlic cloves, salt & process till smooth.
- Place the lamb shoulder in a medium roasting pan & rub half cup of the sauce all over it; let marinate in the fridge for 2 hours or overnight.

- Set the grill temp to 325°F, then keep the lid closed for 15 minutes.
- Fill the roasting pan halfway with water & cover with foil. Cook the lamb for around 3 hours, adding water as needed.
- Remove the foil from the pan & cook for 2 more hours, or till the lamb is tender & brown, spooning the juices on the top as required.
- Remove from the grill & set aside for 20 minutes. Shred the meat & mix it with any leftover liquid from the pan.
- Serve with corn tortillas.

3.8 Lamb Stew

Preparation time: 45 minutes

Cooking time: 2 hours

Servings: 4

Ingredients

- Three large carrots, diced
- One large turnip, diced
- One large parsnip, cubed
- Two tbsp olive oil
- Three lbs. lamb, cut in chunks
- Two bay leaves
- Twelve oz dark beer
- Four garlic cloves, chopped
- 4 tbsp tomato paste
- Two cup beef stock
- Two cup onions, diced
- Two tbsp thyme
- Pepper & salt, to taste

Steps

- Set the grill temp to 450°F, then keep the lid closed for 15 minutes.
- Sprinkle the salt & pepper over the lamb. In a preheated dutch oven heat 2 tbsp of olive oil.
- Arrange the chunks of lamb in the dutch oven in batches, taking care not to overcrowd. Brown all sides of the lamb, around 6-8 minutes.
- Return all the lamb in the pot, add the garlic, tomato paste & cook for another 2 minutes. Add the thyme, beef stock, bay leaves, beer, salt & pepper. Transfer the dutch oven on the grill grate, close the lid & cook for 1 hour.
- Add the onion, turnip, parsnip & carrots & cook for 1 more hour or till the vegetables are tender. Serve with mashed potatoes.

3.9 Irish Braised Lamb

Preparation time: 35 minutes

Cooking time: 3 hours

Servings: 4

Ingredients

- Four lbs. lamb shoulder, cut into chunks
- Two large carrots, cut into chunks
- One sprig rosemary
- Two large potatoes, peeled & cubed
- 4 tbsp all-purpose flour
- Salt & pepper to taste
- Two tbsp olive oil
- Two garlic cloves, chopped
- Half cup red wine
- Two sprigs thyme
- Eight oz bacon, sliced
- One large onion, shopped

- Four cups beef stock
- two bay leaves
- 4 tbsp softened butter

Steps

- Set the grill temp to 350°F, then keep the lid closed for 15 minutes.
- Season the lamb with salt & pepper. In a dutch oven, heat the olive oil over medium heat. Brown the lamb in batches & set it aside.
- Add the bacon & cook, stirring periodically, 15 to 20 minutes. Discard the bacon fat, except for 2 tbsp.
- Add the onions to the dutch oven & cook till wilted. Add the garlic & cook for 1 more min. Return the lamb & bacon to the pan & deglaze with red wine, scraping up all of the browned bits from the bottom with a wooden spatula.
- Add the stock, spices, carrots & potatoes. Bring to a low boil, cover & transfer to the grill grate. Cook for 2 hours or till the lamb is tender & falling apart.

3.10 Lamb Chops with Mediterranean Sauce

Preparation time: 15 minutes

Cooking time: 15 minutes

Servings: 4

Ingredients

- Two garlic cloves, chopped
- Two tbsp soy sauce
- Four lamb chops
- Half cup olive oil
- Four tbsp onion, chopped
- Pepper & salt, to taste
- Two tbsp white wine vinegar
- One tbsp fresh rosemary
- Two tsp french mustard
- One tsp Worcestershire sauce

Steps

- Heat in a small pan one tbsp of olive oil. Stir fry the garlic & onion over medium heat till wilted
- Pour the onion garlic mix into the bowl of a food processor. Add the mustard, soy sauce, rosemary, vinegar & Worcestershire sauce.
- Season with black pepper & start the processor. Slowly pour the residual olive oil till the sauce is properly mixed.
- Set the grill temp to 350°F, then keep the lid closed for 15 minutes.
- Coat all sides of the lamb chops with olive oil & season with salt & pepper, to taste
- Grill the lamb chops for 4 to 6 minutes per side for medium-rare doneness, or more if desired. Serve along with the rosemary sauce.

3.11 Lamb Chops with Mango Chutney

Preparation time: 15 minutes

Cooking time: 10 minutes

Servings: 4

Ingredients

- Three tbsp cilantro, chopped
- Half tsp ground black pepper
- Two tbsp mint, chopped
- One tbsp lime juice

- Salt, to taste
- Two tbsp olive oil
- One Mango, peeled, seeded & chopped
- Three garlic cloves, chopped
- Half tbsp coarse salt
- Six whole Lamb chops, frenched
- Half habanero pepper, seeded & chopped

Steps

- Ask your butcher to french the lamb chops. Otherwise, cut & scrape yourself the flesh & fat off the bone with a sharp knife to make it look like a popsicle.
- Prepare the chutney. In a food processor bowl add the mango, garlic, habanero, cilantro, lime juice. Season with salt & pepper & pulse to combine till required consistency is achieved.
- Set the grill temp to 450°F, then keep the lid closed for 15 minutes.
- Drizzle olive oil over both sides of the lamb chops on a baking sheet. Season with pepper & salt & let rest for 5 to 10 minutes
- Arrange the lamb chops directly on the grill grate. Close the lid & cook for 5 minutes. Turn the meat & cook for additional 3 minutes.
- Take the chops from the grill & let rest for 10 minutes before serving.
- Drizzle chutney over every lamb chop, top with fresh mint & serve.

3.12 Grilled Lamb Rack

Preparation time: 10 minutes

Cooking time: 30 minutes

Servings: 4

Ingredients

- One lamb rack, around 2 lbs.
- Two tsp olive oil
- Eight garlic cloves
- One tsp red wine vinegar
- One thyme bunch
- One tbsp kosher salt

Steps

- In a food processor, combine the garlic, thyme leaves, salt, oil & vinegar. Rub this paste on a full lamb rack.
- Set the grill temp to 450°F, then keep the lid closed for 15 minutes.
- Place the rack of lamb on the grill, fat side down, & cook for a minimum of 20 minutes. Cook for an extra 10 minutes with the flat side facing up. A thermometer inserted into the middle of the lamb meat should read 150-160°F for medium-rare.
- Remove the rack from the grill, cover loosely with aluminum foil & let rest for 10 minutes. Slice the rack into chops & serve.

4.1. Brie Stuffed Turkey Burgers

Preparation time: 15 minutes

Cooking time: 10 minutes

Servings: 8

Ingredients

- Blueberry jalapeño spread, to taste
- One Seven oz bar brie cheese
- 8 Burger buns
- 2 tbsp onion powder
- Salt, to taste
- Two red bell peppers, sliced
- Two handful baby spinach
- Three lbs. ground turkey

Steps

- Set the grill temp to 500°F, then keep the lid closed for 15 minutes.
- Cut the brie bar in 8 parts.
- Place the ground turkey in a mixing bowl, add the onion powder, salt, & knead with your hands to mix.
- Divide the meat into 8 balls. Divide each ball in two halves. Place the first half at the bottom of the burger press, add a portion of crumbled brie, then the second half of the meat ball. Press to shape the burgers.
- Place the burgers directly on the hot grill grate & cook for 5 minutes each side. Place the buns on the grill grate, cut side down, to warm.
- Spread the blueberry jalapeño jam on the bottom buns' halves, then arrange the burgers & top with sliced red peppers & baby spinach. Serve.

4.2 Thanksgiving Smoked Turkey

Preparation time: 1 day

Cooking time: 5 hours

Servings: 8

Ingredients

- One turkey brining kit, including bag, brine mixture, seasoning
- One turkey, around 12 lbs.

Steps

- If you turkey is frozen, defrost it by refrigerating overnight.
- Prepare the brine. Pour 4 cups of water in a pot, add the brine mixture, & bring to a boil. Add this to a gallon of cold water.
- Place the defrosted turkey into the brine bag, add the brine mix & refrigerate for 12 hours.
- Rinse the turkey in cool water, pat dry with paper towel & place it on a roasting pan.
- Rub the turkey with the seasoning from the brine kit. Set the grill temp to 275°F, then keep the lid closed for 15 minutes.
- Put the digital thermometer in the lowest section of the turkey's breast & transfer the turkey in the grill. Cook until the internal

temperature reaches 165°F to 170°F, around 5 hours.

- Remove the turkey from the smoker, let cool & carve as desired.

4.3 Smoked Turkey Legs

Preparation time: 10 minutes

Cooking time: 150 minutes

Servings: 4

Ingredients

- One cup chicken stock
- Four tbsp turkey rub
- Four turkey drumsticks

Steps

- Set the grill temp to 225°F, then keep the lid closed for 15 minutes.
- Pour the chicken stock in a small bowl, add two tsp turkey rub & whisk to combine.
- Arrange the turkey legs on a sheet tray & inject the seasoned stock using a meat injector. Season the exterior of the drumstick with the remaining turkey rub
- Transfer the tray on the grill grate & smoke for one & a half hours.
- Raise the grill temperature to 325° F, then cook the turkey legs for another 45-60 minutes, or till the internal temperature reaches 170° F.
- Remove the turkey legs from the grill, cover loosely with aluminum foil & let rest for 10 minutes before serving.

4.4 Cajun Butter Spatchcocked Turkey

Preparation time: 30 minutes

Cooking time: 3 hours

Servings: 8

Ingredients

Cajun Butter

- One cup butter
- Three tsp cayenne powder
- Two tsp dark sugar
- Halt tsp garlic powder
- Half tsp onion powder
- One tsp thyme, chopped
- Half tsp black pepper

Main

- Turkey rub, to taste
- One brined spatchcocked turkey, around 12 lbs.

Steps

- Prepare the Cajun butter. In a small bowl whisk thoroughly the softened butter with the other ingredients, until properly combined.
- Set the grill temp to 300°F, then keep the lid closed for 15 minutes.
- In your turkey is not brined, check recipe 4.2 for further instructions. Season the turkey with turkey rub & inject with Cajun butter with the help of a meat injector.
- Arrange the turkey breast side up on the grill grates, close the lid & cook till the internal temperature hits 165°F, around three hours.
- Remove the turkey from the grill, let rest for 30 minutes & carve as desired.

4.5 Bacon Lattice Turkey

Preparation time: 30 minutes

Cooking time: 3 hours

Servings: 8

Ingredients

- Two apples, cored peeled & diced
- Twelve slices bacon
- Two celery sticks, diced
- One tbsp dried herb mix

* One onion, sliced
* Black pepper, to taste
* One tbsp chicken rub
* One brined turkey, around 12 lbs.

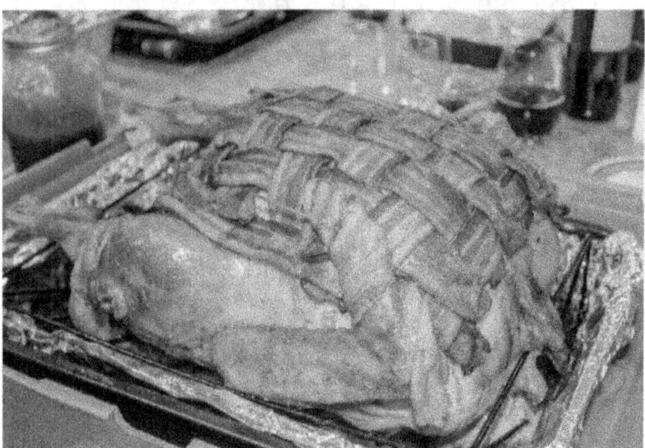

* Set the grill temp to 300°F, then keep the lid closed for 15 minutes.
* Wash the turkey under running water & pat dry with paper towels.
* Stuff the turkey with apples, celery & onion.
* In a small bowl mix the herb mix, chicken rub & pepper. Season the entire turkey generously with the mixture.
* Create a lattice pattern with the bacon slices on a sheet of parchment paper. Flip the sheet & cover the turkey breasts with the bacon.
* Arrange the turkey on a roasting pan, transfer to the grill grate, close the lid & cook until the internal breast temperature reaches 165°F to 170°F, around 3 hours.
* Remove the turkey from the grill, let rest for 30 minutes & carve as desired.

4.6 Pepper & Onion Turkey Burgers

Preparation time: 45 minutes

Cooking time: 15 minutes

Servings: 4

Ingredients

* Four tbsp red onion, chopped
* One jalapeño pepper, chopped
* One tbsp chicken rub
* One handful baby spinach
* Sixteen oz turkey, ground
* Four slices cheddar cheese

Steps

* Set the grill temp to 400°F, then keep the lid closed for 15 minutes.
* Place the ground turkey in a mixing bowl & season generously with the chicken rub.
* Add the chopped jalapeño pepper, the chopped onion & mix with your hands. Cover with cling film & refrigerate for 30 minutes to let the flavors blend.
* Divide the seasoned turkey in four meatballs. Flatten the balls with your hands or use a burger press.
* Transfer the patties to the grill grate & cook for around 15 minutes, turning once.
* When the meat is almost done, top each patty with a slice of cheddar & place the buns on the grill grate, cut side down. Keep cooking until the cheese is melted.
* Remove the turkey patties & buns from the grill. Top the turkey patties with baby spinach & serve.

4.7 Mayonnaise & Herbs Turkey

Preparation time: 20 minutes

Cooking time: 4 hours

Servings: 8

Ingredients

* One cup mayonnaise
* 4 tbsp yellow mustard
* One handful fresh herbs of your choice, chopped
* One tbsp sugar
* One turkey, around 12 lbs.
* Pepper & salt, to taste

- Half cup butter, softened
- Four tbsp thyme
- Half cup sage

Steps

- Set the grill temp to 425°F, then keep the lid closed for 15 minutes.
- Combine the mayonnaise, mustard, sugar & chopped herbs in a bowl. Whisk thoroughly to blend.
- Rub the mayonnaise mustard mixture all over the turkey. Season with pepper & salt, also in the cavity.
- Stuff the cavity of the turkey with thyme, butter, & age. Using kitchen twine, truss the legs & wings.
- Arrange the turkey on a roasting pan, transfer to the grill grate, close the lid & cook for 30-45 minutes, or till the skin becomes golden brown.
- Lower the grill temperature to 350°F & keep cooking until the internal breast temperature reaches 165°F.
- Remove the turkey from the grill, cover loosely with aluminum foil & let rest for about 10-15 minutes. Carve as desired & serve.

4.8 Smoked Turkey Jerky

Preparation time: 8 hours

Cooking time: 4 hours

Servings: 6

Ingredients

- Half cup soy sauce
- Two tbsp honey
- Two tbsp chinese garlic chili sauce
- Two tbsp lime juice
- One tbsp Morton curing salt
- Four lbs. turkey breast

Steps

- Combine the curing salt, soy sauce, lime juice, chili garlic paste, & honey in a mixing bowl. Add a quarter cup of water & whisk thoroughly. Cut the turkey around the grain in 1/4-inch slices. Take care to remove any fat, connective tissue & membrane.
- Fill a big zip top plastic bag halfway with the turkey slices. Add the marinade mix & massage the bag to properly season all the meat. Close the bag & refrigerate overnight.
- Set the grill temp to 180°F, then keep the lid closed for 15 minutes.
- Remove the turkey from the bag & discard the marinade. Carefully pat dry any single turkey slice with paper towels. Arrange the slice in a single layer on a big cookie sheet & transfer on the grill grate. Close the lid.
- Smoke about 3 hours, keep in mind that the meat must be crispy outside but still pliable & chewy when bent.
- Remove the turkey from the grill & transfer to a zip top plastic bag. Let rest at room temp for one hour, squeeze the air out of the bag & store in the fridge for up to two weeks.

4.9 Drunken Turkey Legs

Preparation time: 15 minutes

Cooking time: 2 hours

Servings: 4

Ingredients

- One bottle chili sauce
- Half cup butter, softened
- One cup dark sugar

- Half cup Bourbon whiskey
- Three garlic cloves, minced
- One tsp Cajun seasoning
- Half cup chicken stock
- Six large turkey drumsticks

Steps

- Combine all ingredients in a saucepan, excluding the turkey drumsticks. Bring the mixture to a simmer, whisk to dissolve the sugar & turn the heat off. Allow cooling before pouring the marinade in a zip top bag with the turkey drumsticks. Refrigerate overnight.
- Remove the drumsticks from the bag & save the marinade. Bring the marinade to a boil & let cool.
- In a bowl dilute half of the marinade with the chicken stock. Inject the mixture in the turkey drumstick using a meat injector. Reserve the other half marinade for basting.
- Set the grill temp to 250°F, then keep the lid closed for 15 minutes.
- Place the turkey drumsticks on grill grate, then cook about 2 - 3 hours, depending on the size of turkey legs, or until the internal temperature reaches 165° F. Baste the meat every 45 minutes using the reserved marinade.

4.10 Turkey Gravy on the Grill

Preparation time: 20 minutes

Cooking time: 2 hours

Servings: 8

Ingredients

- One turkey neck
- Two large onions, chopped
- Four stalks celery, chopped
- Four large fresh carrots, chopped
- Eight garlic cloves, chopped
- Eight thyme sprigs
- One quart chicken stock

- One tsp salt
- One tsp black pepper
- One stick butter
- One cup all-purpose flour

Steps

- Set the grill temp to 350°F, then keep the lid closed for 15 minutes.
- Place the thyme, turkey neck, garlic, onions, carrots, & celery in a deep skillet. Season with pepper, salt & pour the chicken stock.
- Transfer the skillet to the grill grate & cook for around 2 hours.
- Pour the drippings in the saucepan & set the grill to low heat.
- In a saucepan placed on the grill grate, prepare a roux whisking together the butter & flour until golden brown.
- Add the turkey drippings to the roux, bring them to a boil, season to taste with pepper & salt. Serve hot.

4.11 Bacon Stuffed Turkey Breast

Preparation time: 20 minutes

Cooking time: 40 minutes

Servings: 6

Ingredients

- One turkey breast, boneless
- Four thick bacon strips, diced
- One cup cremini mushrooms, chopped
- One bunch scallions, chopped
- Two tbsp white wine
- Four tbsp Panko breadcrumbs
- Black pepper, to taste
- Salt, to taste

Steps

- Set the grill temp to 375°F, then keep the lid closed for 15 minutes.

- Divide the turkey breast in two, then butterfly each half cutting horizontally, taking not to cut all the way through.
- Stir fry the bacon in a pan until crispy. Put the bacon aside leaving the fat in the pan. Sauté the mushrooms in the bacon fat until wilted. Adding the scallions, cook for 2 more minutes & add the white wine. When all the wine is evaporated, season with pepper & salt. Add the breadcrumbs, stir well & turn off the heat.
- Spread the cooled stuffing over the turkey breasts. Tightly roll the turkey breasts & tie them with butcher's twine. Tuck the turkey breasts' ends under & tie lengthwise.
- Season the turkey breast with pepper & salt, transfer to the grill grate & cook for about 40 minutes or until the internal temperature reaches 165°F. Remove the turkey from the grill, cover loosely with foil & let rest for 10 minutes. Slice & serve.

4.12 Oriental Lettuce-Wrapped Turkey Burgers

Preparation time: 15 minutes

Cooking time: 15 minutes

Servings: 4

Ingredients

- Three tbsp mayonnaise
- One tbsp Sriracha hot sauce
- One lb. turkey, ground
- Half cup panko breadcrumbs
- Four tablespoons cilantro, chopped
- Three garlic cloves, chopped
- Two scallions, chopped
- Three tbsp Soy sauce
- One tbsp sesame oil
- One tbsp fresh ginger, grated
- One tsp red pepper flakes
- One head iceberg lettuce
- One tomato, sliced
- One red onion, sliced

Steps

- Set the grill temp to 500°F, then keep the lid closed for 15 minutes.
- Combine mayonnaise & Sriracha hot sauce, then set aside.
- In a mixing bowl combine the meat, breadcrumbs, cilantro, garlic, scallions, soy sauce, sesame oil, ginger & pepper flakes. Knead with your hands until properly combined.
- Divide the mix in four & form the patties with your hands or use a burger press if you like.
- Grill your burgers for 5-7 minutes each side or until an instant thermometer reads a 165° F internal temperature.
- Take a leaf of lettuce & place the burger in the center. Top with sliced tomato, red onion & a dollop of Sriracha mayonnaise.
- Wrap the burger in the lettuce leaf & serve.

5.1 Smoky Burgers

Preparation time: 15 minutes

Cooking time: 2 hours

Servings: 8

Ingredients

- Two lbs. beef, ground
- One tbs Worcestershire sauce
- Two tbsp beef rub

Steps

- Combine the ground beef, Worcestershire sauce, & beef rub in a mixing bowl. Knead with your hands to spread the flavors.
- Create eight hamburger patties with the beef mixture. You can shape the patties with your hands or use a burger press.
- Set the grill temp to 180°F, then keep the lid closed for 15 minutes.
- Transfer the burgers on the grill grate & smoke for about 2 hours.
- Remove the burgers from the grill & serve with your favorite toppings.

5.2 Marinated Beef Ribs

Preparation time: 15 minutes

Cooking time: 2 hours

Servings: 8

Ingredients

- Four racks of beef back ribs
- Beef rub, to taste
- One cup white wine
- Four tbsp olive oil
- Two tbsp Worcestershire sauce
- Two tbsp french mustard
- One tbsp salt
- One tsp black pepper
- Three garlic cloves, chopped
- One small onion, chopped
- One bay leaf, crumbled

Steps

- Arrange the ribs inside a large zip top bag.
- Prepare the marinade. Whisk together pepper, salt, wine, mustard, olive oil, & Worcestershire sauce in a mixing bowl. Add the onion, garlic, & bay leaf, mix & pour this marinade in the zip top bag along with the ribs. Massage the bag to let the flavors combine.
- Refrigerate the ribs overnight. Flip the bag several time to ensure that the beef is uniformly marinated.
- Take the ribs out of the bag & discard the marinade. Pat the ribs dry with paper towels & generously season with beef rub on all sides.
- Set the grill temp to 250°F, then keep the lid closed for 15 minutes.
- Place the ribs bone side down directly on the grill grate. Cook for around 5 hours or the internal temperature reaches 200°F. Serve.

5.3 Dark Beer-Braised Beef Ribs

Preparation time: 10 minutes

Cooking time: 4 hours

Servings: 4

Ingredients

- Two racks back beef ribs
- Kosher Salt, to taste
- Black Pepper, to taste
- Garlic powder, to taste
- One can dark beer
- BBQ sauce, for serving

Steps

- In a small bowl mix salt, pepper & garlic powder. Season both sides of the rib racks with the mixture. Place the ribs in a foil tray & refrigerate 2 hours.
- Set the grill temp to 165°F, then keep the lid closed for 15 minutes.
- Place the ribs in a roasting pan over the grill grate & then smoke for one hour. Pour the beer in the pan, taking care not to wash off the ribs seasoning & cover the pan with aluminum foil.
- Raise the grill temperature to 250°F & steam the ribs for another 3 hours, or until the beef very tender.
- Take the pan off the grill & remove the foil carefully. Discard the cooking liquid & serve the ribs with your favorite BBQ sauce.

5.4 Oriental Beef Skewers

Preparation time: 1 hour

Cooking time: 8 minutes

Servings: 6

Ingredients

- Two lbs. flat iron steak
- Two cups marinade for carne asada
- Three garlic cloves, chopped
- Two scallions, chopped
- Two medium yellow bell peppers, cubed
- Oriental peanut sauce, for serving
- 4 tbsp peanuts, chopped
- 2 limes, wedged

Steps

- Slice the steak in 1/3-inch slices against the grain. Place the slices in a zip top bag.

- Pour the marinade into the bag, add the garlic & scallions & massage the meat to let the flavors combine. Refrigerate for 1 hour.
- Remove the meat strips from the marinade, discarding all the vegetables. Thread every piece on a skewer & place a pepper square at the end.
- Set the grill temp to 500°F, then keep the lid closed for 15 minutes.
- Grill each skewer for 3-4 minutes per side, turning once.
- Transfer the skewers to a serving platter. Drizzle with the peanut sauce & a sprinkle of peanuts. Serve with lime wedges as a garnish.

5.5 Root Beer BBQ Short Ribs

Preparation time: 15 minutes

Cooking time: 3 hours

Servings: 4

Ingredients

- Four tbsp chili sauce
- Four tbsp BBQ Sauce
- One cup root beer
- One tbsp thyme
- One large onion, sliced
- Four lbs. bone-In short ribs
- Salt, to taste
- Black Pepper, to taste

Steps

- Combine in a bowl the root beer, BBQ sauce, chili sauce & thyme leaves. Whisk to mix.

- Season with salt & pepper the ribs, on both sides.
- Spread the onions on the bottom of a roasting dish. Arrange the ribs on top, in a single layer. Pour the root beer mix in the dish, taking care not to wash off the seasoning from the ribs. Tightly wrap with aluminum foil.
- Set the grill temp to 300°F, then keep the lid closed for 15 minutes.
- Transfer the dish to the grill grate & cook for 2-3 hours, until the ribs are soft but not falling off the bones.
- Take the platter from the grill & carefully remove the foil.
- Serve the ribs over mashed potatoes.

5.6 Chili Beef Jerky

Preparation time: 10 minutes

Cooking time: 4 hours

Servings: 4

Ingredients

- One cup chili sauce
- Half cup beer
- Two tbsp soy sauce
- One tbsp Worcestershire sauce
- Two tbsp. Morton curing salt
- One tbsp jalapeño pickled peppers, chopped
- Two lbs. flank steak, sliced into 1/4-inch-thick slices

Steps

- Prepare the marinade. Combine the curing salt, soy sauce, chili sauce, Worcestershire sauce, beer, & jalapeños into a mixing bowl.
- Place the beef slices in a large top zip bag. Pour the marinade in the bag & massage to evenly spread the flavors. Refrigerate overnight.
- Set the grill temp to 165°F, then keep the lid closed for 15 minutes.
- Remove the beef from the bag & discard the marinade. Pat the meat dry with paper towels.
- Arrange the beef in a single layer directly on the grill grate.

- Smoke the jerky for 4-5 hours, or till dried but still chewy & pliable.
- Remove the jerky from the grill, let cool a bit & store in a zip top bag.
- Let sit at room temperature for one hour, then squeeze the air out of the bag & store the jerky in the refrigerator for up to two weeks.

5.7 Reuben Sandwich

Preparation time: 10 minutes

Cooking time: 10 minutes

Servings: 4

Ingredients

- Two cups mayonnaise
- Half cup ketchup
- Four tbsp pickle relish
- Two tbsp chicken rub
- Four lbs. corned beef, thinly sliced
- Three cups sauerkraut
- Ten slices swiss cheese
- Ten slices rye bread
- Six tbsp butter, softened

Steps

- Set the grill temp to 165°F, then keep the lid closed for 15 minutes.
- Prepare the sauce. In a mixing bowl, whisk together the relish, ketchup, mayonnaise, & chicken rub until well blended.
- Butter one side of the bread slices. Spread sauce on the other side & cover with sauerkraut, corned beef, & two swiss cheese slices. Top with another buttered slice of bread.
- Place the sandwiches directly on the hot grill & cook for about 5 minutes. Flip the sandwiches with a spatula, then cook for another 5 minutes, or till the bread is toasted & the cheese is melted.
- Remove the sandwiches from the grill, cut in half & serve.

5.8 Vietnamese Beef Jerky

Preparation time: 20 minutes

Cooking time: 4 hours

Servings: 6

Ingredients

- Two lbs. sirloin or rump roast
- Two garlic cloves, chopped
- One stalk fresh lemongrass
- Two tbsp ginger, chopped
- Half cup soy sauce
- Three tbsp sugar
- Two tbsp fish sauce
- Two tsp red pepper flakes
- Half tsp pink curing salt

Steps

- Remove all the fat from meat & cut this into thin slices against all the grain with a sharp chef's knife. It gets easier if the beef is semi-frozen. Fill a big resealable bag halfway with the meat.
- Prepare the marinade. Combine the pink curing salt, garlic, pepper flakes, lemongrass, fish sauce, ginger, soy sauce in a food processor bowl. Pulse until smooth.
- Pour the marinade on the meat, then massage the bag until the meat slices are uniformly covered. Refrigerate overnight flipping the bag a couple of time.
- Set the grill temp to 165°F, then keep the lid closed for 15 minutes.

- Drain that meat, pat dry with paper towels & discard the marinade. Arrange the beef strips in a single layer directly on the grill grate. Smoke for 4 hours or until the meat is dried but still pliable.
- Remove the jerky from the grill, let cool a bit & store in a zip top bag.
- Let sit at room temperature for one hour, then squeeze the air out of the bag & store the jerky in the refrigerator for up to two weeks.

5.9 Prime Rib Roast with Mustard & Herbs

Preparation time: 15 minutes

Cooking time: 3 hours

Servings: 8

Ingredients

- One prime-rib roast, bone-in
- Olive oil, to taste
- Kosher salt, to taste
- Black Pepper, to taste
- One cup french mustard
- One cup mixed dried herbs

Steps

- Coat the meat with olive oil. Season on all sides with salt & pepper. Then, uniformly brush both sides with french mustard & generously sprinkle with mixed dried herbs. Let rest the meat in the refrigerator, without covering, for 1 day.
- Set the grill temp to 325°F, then keep the lid closed for 15 minutes. Cook the prime-rib roast for around 3 hours, fat side up. When the internal temperature hits 110°F, remove the roast from the grill.
- Cover the roast with foil & let rest for 1 hour. The internal temperature will continue to rise till around 130°F, for medium-rare. Carve the roast following the bones & serve.

5.10 Rib Eyes with Hasselback Sweet Potatoes

Preparation time: 15 minutes

Servings: 4

Ingredients

- Two rib eye steaks, bone in
- Four sweet potatoes
- Olive oil, as needed
- Salt, to taste
- Pepper, to taste

Steps

- Take the rob eye steaks out from the refrigerator an hour before starting to cook.
- Set the grill temp to 325°F, then keep the lid closed for 15 minutes.
- Cut the potatoes into one-eighth-inch slices with the sharp knife, just going three-quarters of the way through. You may place two chopsticks on the side of the potato for easier cutting.
- Arrange the sliced potatoes on a cookie sheet. Drizzle with olive oil & sprinkle with pepper & salt to taste. Put the sheet on the grill grates & cook for around 1 hour, until the potatoes are cooked & nicely browned.
- While the potatoes are cooking, coat the steaks in olive oil & season generously with pepper & salt on both sides.
- Put the steaks onto the grill grate when the sweet potatoes are almost done & cook until the internal temperature hits 130°F for medium, around 5 minutes each side.
- Remove the steaks from the grill, cover with foil an let rest for 10 minutes.
- Slice the steaks across the grain & arrange on a serving platter along with the potatoes. Serve.

5.11 Cajun Stuffed Peppers

Preparation time: 15 minutes

Cooking time: 40 minutes

Servings: 6

Ingredients

- Six large red bell peppers
- One lb. beef, ground
- Two tbsp olive oil
- One small onion, diced
- Two garlic cloves, chopped
- Two tbsp Cajun rub
- 1 cup salsa
- Two cups rice, cooked
- One cup black beans, drained
- One cup fresh corn
- Two cups Monterey Jack cheese, shredded
- Salt & pepper, to taste

Steps

- Wash the bell peppers under running water. Cut in half, remove the stems & remove ribs & seeds with a paring knife.
- In a big pan, stir fry the ground beef with the olive oil, breaking any lump with a wooden spatula.
- Add the garlic & onion. Cook till the flavors are combined, around 5 minutes. Add the Cajun rub, corn, salsa, black beans & rice. Season with salt & pepper & let cool. Stuff each half of pepper with the mix.
- Set the grill temp to 350°F, then keep the lid closed for 15 minutes.
- Arrange the peppers, stuffed side up, directly onto grill grate, & bake for about 40 minutes.
- Top the peppers with shredded Monterey Jack, cook for another 5 minutes or to melt the cheese & serve.

5.12 Smoked Meatball Rolls

Preparation time: 15 minutes

Cooking time: 50 minutes

Servings: 4

Ingredients

- One egg
- One third cup milk
- Two tbsp Worcestershire sauce
- Half cup panko breadcrumbs
- One tbsp beef rub
- One & half lbs. beef, ground
- One small onion, minced
- Black pepper, to taste
- Two garlic cloves, minced

- One jar marinara sauce
- Four baguettes
- Two cups Provolone cheese, shredded

Steps

- Beat the egg with a whisk in a mixing bowl. Add the Worcestershire sauce, milk, beef rub & breadcrumbs & mix well.
- In another bowl mix the black pepper, garlic, onion, & ground beef. Knead with your hands. Add egg mixture & mix again till properly combined.
- If the mix seems too dry, Add a little milk. In it seems too wet, add some breadcrumbs. Shape the mix into golf ball-sized spheres.
- Set the grill temp to 325°F, then keep the lid closed for 15 minutes.
- Place the meatballs onto the grill grate directly. Cook for around 30 minutes, till the balls are thoroughly done.
- Meanwhile, heat the marinara sauce into a saucepan. When the meatballs are ready, transfer to the pan & simmer in the sauce for 10 minutes.
- Divide the meatballs between the baguettes, top generously with shredded provolone cheese, wrap each single baguette in foil & heat for 10 minutes on the hot grill grates.
- Take the baguettes from the grill, remove the foil & serve.

6.1 BBQ Chicken Bacon Rolls

Preparation time: 15 minutes

Cooking time: 1 hour

Servings: 8

Ingredients

- One whole chicken
- Two tbsp chicken rub
- Half lb. bacon, sliced
- 8 ciabatta buns
- One butter lettuce head
- Two sliced tomatoes
- Two avocadoes
- Eight slices swiss cheese
- BBQ sauce, to taste
- Ranch dressing, to taste

Steps

- Set the grill temp to 325°F, then keep the lid closed for 15 mins.
- Season the whole chicken with pepper & salt. generously sprinkle with chicken rub.
- Place the chicken directly on the grill grate & cook for 60 to 90 mins, till the internal breast temperature hits 160°F
- Season one side of the bacon slices with chicken rub while the chicken is grilling.

Place the slice on the grill grates, next to the chicken & cook for around 30 minutes, till bacon is crispy.

- Remove the chicken from the grill & let cool until room temperature.
- Cut off the dark meat from the chicken thighs, remove the breast & slice. Peel, core & slice the avocadoes, slice the tomatoes, prepare the lettuce leaves.
- Halve the ciabatta buns, spread BBQ sauce, top with lettuce, sliced chicken, bacon, avocado, cheese, tomato, & ranch dressing. Serve.

6.2 Smoked Whole Chicken

Preparation time: 15 minutes

Cooking time: 3 hours

Servings: 4

Ingredients

Brine

- One cup salt
- Two tbsp. brown sugar
- Two garlic cloves, chopped
- Two springs thyme
- Two springs rosemary

Main

- One whole chicken
- One lemon, halved
- One bulb garlic, halved
- Two tbsp olive oil
- One tbsp. Lemon Zest

Seasoning

- Four tsp kosher salt
- Four tsp garlic powder
- One tsp onion powder
- One tsp dried thyme
- One tsp smoked paprika

- One tsp dried parsley
- One tsp black pepper
- One tsp coriander seeds, crushed

- Prepare the brine. Pour 4 cups water in a pot, add sugar, garlic, salt, & herbs & carry to a simmer. Stir until the salt has dissolved.
- Add 8 cups of cool water & turn off the heat. Place the chicken in a big resealable bag, pour the brine & refrigerate overnight.
- Combine all the seasoning ingredients in a bowl.
- Set the grill temp to 225°F, then keep the lid closed for 15 mins.
- Using paper towels, pat the chicken dry after removing it from the brine.
- Drizzle oil all over the chicken. Rubbed the chicken with 2 tbsp of the prepared seasoning & fill the bird's cavity with both halves of the garlic bulb & half lemon.
- Transfer the chicken to the grill grates & smoke until the internal breast temperature hits 170°F around 3 hours.
- Remove the chicken from the grill, cover with foil & let rest 10 minutes. Carve as desired & serve.

6.3 Grilled Chicken with Hot Salsa

Preparation time: 10 minutes

Cooking time: 45 minutes

Servings: 6

Ingredients

Main

- Six whole chicken legs, thighs & drumsticks
- Two tbsp olive oil
- One tbsp smoked paprika
- One tsp ground coriander
- Zest of one lime
- One tsp sea salt
- One tsp black pepper

Hot Salsa

- Four jalapeños
- Four garlic cloves
- Six spring fresh cilantro
- Two green onions
- One tbsp lime juice
- Two tbsp maple syrup
- Half cup white wine vinegar
- One tsp sea salt

- Prepare the chicken. In a big resealable bag combine the chicken, smoked paprika, olive oil, coriander, pepper, lime zest, & sea salt. Massage the bag to evenly spread the seasoning & refrigerate for 4 hours.
- Set the grill temp to 350°F, then keep the lid closed for 15 mins.
- Place the chicken, skin side up, directly on grill grates. Cook for 40 minutes, or until the chicken hits an internal temperature of 165°F
- Prepare the hot salsa while the chicken is cooking. Place the peppers on the grill grates along with the chicken & cook till slightly charred, approximately 25 minutes. Remove the peppers, then combine with the other salsa ingredients in a blender. Pulse till the mixture is almost smooth. Season to taste.
- Remove the chicken from the grill, arrange on a serving platter & serve along with the hot salsa.

6.4 Chicken & Bacon Hot Casserole

Preparation time: 25 minutes

Cooking time: 50 minutes

Servings: 4

Ingredients

- Two tbsp butter
- Four tbsp all-purpose flour
- Two cans cream of chicken soup

- Two cups milk
- Two medium onions, chopped
- One lb. chicken thighs, boned
- Four jalapeño peppers, chopped
- Half tsp dried thyme
- Salt & pepper, to taste
- One cup bacon, chopped

- Set the grill temp to 400°F, then keep the lid closed for 15 mins.
- Melt the butter in a pan over medium heat, then whisk in the flour.
- Whisk the milk in the pan, then the creamy soup. Continue whisking until the mixture thickens.
- Add the thyme, chicken, peppers. Cook for around 15 minutes, until the chicken is properly cooked.
- Stir in the bacon & season with salt & pepper to taste.
- Pour the mixture into an oven-proof casserole pan & top with the tater.
- Transfer the casserole to the grill grate & cook for around 35 mins, until golden brown. Serve.

6.5 Yogurt Chicken Kebabs

Preparation time: 10 minutes

Cooking time: 20 minutes

Servings: 4

Ingredients

Marinade

- Two cups greek yogurt
- One cup cilantro, chopped
- Juice of two limes
- Three garlic cloves, chopped
- One tsp turmeric
- One tsp curry powder
- One tsp ground cumin
- Salt & Pepper, to taste

Main

- Two lbs. chicken thighs, boned, skin on.

Steps

- Whisk together all the marinade ingredients in a bowl. Cut the chicken thighs in bite-sized chunks, add to the marinade & mix well. Cover with cling film & refrigerate overnight.
- Set the grill temp to 360°F, then keep the lid closed for 15 mins.
- Skewer the chicken; you should get 8 skewers.
- Put the skewers directly on the grill grate & cook for 10 to 15 mins, turning once, till the chicken is properly done.
- Take the skewers from the grill, let cool a bit & serve.

6.6 Grilled Thai Chicken

Preparation time: 1 hour

Cooking time: 25 minutes

Servings: 6

Ingredients

- Four tbsp soy sauce
- Three tbsp dark sugar
- Two tbsp lime juice
- Two tbsp oil
- One tsp red curry paste
- Two garlic cloves, chopped
- One tsp dried lemon grass

- One tsp fresh ginger, chopped
- One jalapeño pepper, chopped
- Three lbs. chicken breasts, skinned
- Cilantro, for garnish
- Fresh coconut flakes, for garnish

- Prepare the marinade. In a mixing bowl, combine soy sauce, dark sugar, lime juice, oil, curry paste, garlic, lemon grass, ginger & jalapeño.
- Combine the marinade & the chicken breasts in a large zip top bag. Marinate the chicken for 1 to 4 hours.
- Set the grill temp to 450°F, then keep the lid closed for 15 mins.
- Remove the chicken from the marinade & place it on the grill grate.
- Cook the chicken breasts for about 12 mins to each side, until properly done.
- Remove the chicken from the grill, cover with foil & let rest for 5 minutes.
- Sprinkle with chopped cilantro & coconut flakes. Serve.

6.7 Beer & Serrano Wings

Preparation time: 10 minutes

Cooking time: 45 minutes

Servings: 4

Ingredients

- Four lbs. chicken wings
- One can beer
- Two tsp red pepper flakes
- Two tbsp chicken Rub
- One lb. serrano pepper
- Four garlic cloves
- One tbsp fresh oregano
- One tbsp fresh basil
- Half tsp celery salt
- Half tsp black pepper
- One cup white wine vinegar

Steps

- Trim the wings into drumettes & flats. Discard the rib tips. Combine the wings, red pepper flakes & beer in a bowl. Cover with cling film & refrigerate overnight.
- Remove the wings & from the marinade & pat dry with. Discard the marinade.
- Season the wings with the chicken rub.
- Set the grill temp to 325°F, then keep the lid closed for 15 mins.
- Place the wings directly on the grill grate. Also arrange the serrano peppers. Flip the peppers after 10 minutes & grill for another 5 minutes, till the skin is lightly charred.
- Remove the peppers from the grill & flip the chicken wings, Grill the wings for another 20 to 25 minutes while you prepare the hot sauce.
- Remove the stems from the peppers & transfer to a food processor along with garlic, celery salt, oregano, basil, & black pepper.
- Start processing & steadily add the vinegar. Process until desired consistency is reached.
- Baste the wings with the hot sauce for the last 5 minutes of cooking.
- Remove the wings from the grill, arrange on a serving platter & serve along with the leftover hot sauce.

6.8 BBQ Spatchcocked Chicken

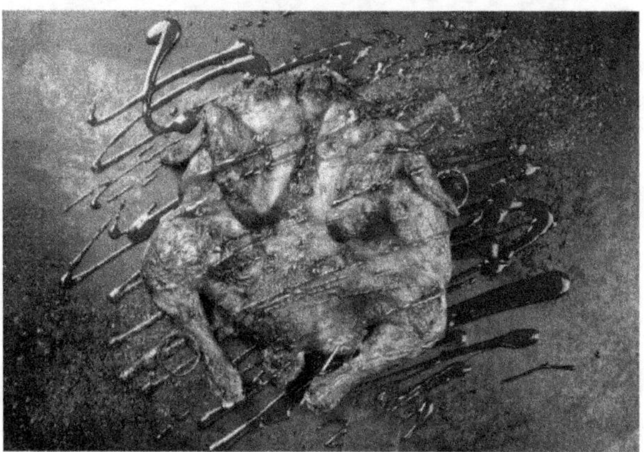

Preparation time: 20 minutes

Ingredients

- One whole chicken
- Four tbsp chicken rub
- Two tbsp olive oil
- Hot BBQ sauce, to taste.

Steps

- Set the grill temp to 375°F, then keep the lid closed for 15 mins.
- To open the bird, cut both sides of the backbone with shears & remove.
- Cut the breastbone on the other side & press to flatten. This will allow the chicken to cook evenly. Brush all sides of the chicken with olive oil & season with chicken rub.
- Transfer the chicken to the grill grate, skin side up, & cook for 30 to 40 minutes. The internal breast temperature should hit 160°F.
- Baste chicken with BBQ sauce in the last few mins of cooking & roast for another 2 minutes to set the glaze. Remove the chicken from the grill, cover with foil & let rest for 5 mins. Carve as desired & serve.

6.9 Tikka Drumsticks

Preparation time: 10 minutes

Cooking time: 45 minutes

Servings: 6

Ingredients

Marinade

- Four tbsp olive oil
- One tbsp smoked paprika
- One tbsp garam masala
- One tbsp ground cumin
- One tbsp ground coriander
- One tsp turmeric
- One tsp cayenne pepper
- Juice of half lemon
- Half onion, diced
- One inch fresh ginger, chopped
- Six garlic cloves, chopped

Curry yogurt

- Two cups greek yogurt
- One pinch sea salt
- One tsp curry powder
- One tbsp lime juice

Main

- Twelve chicken drumsticks
- Cilantro, to taste
- Half red onion, sliced
- One lime, wedged
- Two red chilies, sliced

Steps

- Prepare the marinade. Combine all the marinade ingredients in a food processor & pulse to combine until smooth.
- Place the chicken in a big resealable plastic bag. Add in the marinade & massage until the drumsticks are evenly covered. Refrigerate overnight.
- Set the grill temp to 500°F, then keep the lid closed for 15 minutes.
- Put the chicken directly on the grill grate & cook for around 45 minutes, until crispy & golden brown.
- Prepare the curry yogurt. Mix all the ingredients in a small bowl & stir thoroughly. Keep refrigerated until ready to serve.
- Arrange the drumsticks in a serving platter, scatter cilantro, red chilies & sliced red onion on top. Serve with lime wedges & the curry yogurt.

6.10 Orange Mustard Chicken

Preparation time: 15 minutes

Cooking time: 45 minutes

Servings: 4

Ingredients

- One spatchcocked chicken
- Four tbsp olive oil
- Juice of two oranges
- Zest of one orange
- Two tsp french mustard
- Two tbsp rosemary, chopped
- Kosher salt, to taste

Steps

- If you cannot find a spatchcocked chicken, do it yourself. Cut with shears both side of the backbone & discard it. Flip the bird, cut the breastbone & press to flatten. Rinse the chicken & pat dry with paper towels.
- Prepare the marinade. Combine all the ingredients (except the chicken) in a bowl & whisk thoroughly to combine.
- Place the chicken in a big resealable bag. Pour the marinade, close the bag & massage the chicken to spread the flavors. Refrigerate overnight, flipping the bag a couple of times.
- Set the grill temp to 350°F, then keep the lid closed for 15 minutes.
- Take out the chicken from the marinade, pat dry with paper towels & arrange directly on the grill grate, skin-side down. Discard the marinade.
- Cook for around 30 minutes, until the skin is crispy & nicely browned, then flip. Grill the chicken for 5 to 15 more minutes, until the internal breast temperature hits 165°F. Remove the chicken from the grill, let rest for 5 minutes & carve as desired.

6.11 Ancho Chile BBQ Drumsticks

Preparation time: 15 minutes

Cooking time: 2 hours

Servings: 4

Ingredients

- One tbsp ancho chile powder
- Two tbsp brown sugar
- Half tbsp ground coffee
- Half tsp ground cumin
- Zest of one lime
- Kosher salt, to taste
- Two tbsp olive oil
- Eight chicken drumsticks
- BBQ sauce, to taste
- One Lime, wedged
- Parsley, to serve

Steps

- Coat the drumsticks in olive oil. In a small bowl, combine the ancho chili powder, cumin, brown sugar, lime zest, coffee & salt.
- Sprinkle the dry rub on the chicken & massage it thoroughly. Place the drumstick in a bowl, cover with cling film & refrigerate overnight.
- Set the grill temp to 180°F, then keep the lid closed for 15 minutes.
- Arrange the drumstick on the grill grate & smoke for 1 hour.
- Raise the grill temperature to 360°F. Cook for another hour, until the chicken internal temperature reaches 165°F.
- In the last 10 minutes of cooking, spread BBQ sauce on the drumstick & let the glaze form. Remove from the grill, sprinkle with chopped parsley & serve with lime wedges.

6.12 Bacon Wrapped Chicken Skewers

Preparation time: 15 minutes

Cooking time: 20 minutes

Servings: 6

Ingredients

- Half cup Ranch dressing
- Half tsp garlic powder
- Half tbsp chili sauce
- Half tsp dried oregano
- Sixteen oz chicken breast, cubed
- One red onion, wedged
- One green bell pepper, wedges
- Ten strips bacon, sliced

Steps

- Combine in a bowl the ranch dressing, chili sauce, garlic powder & oregano. Add the chicken cubes & toss well to coat. Cover with cling film & refrigerate for 3 hours.
- Set the grill temp to 500°F, then keep the lid closed for 15 minutes.
- Assemble the skewers. Start with an onion wedge, a pepper wedge, then a cube of chicken wrapped in a piece of bacon. Alternate the ingredients until finished. Try to prepare smaller skewers, as they cook more evenly & are easily flipped.
- Arrange the skewers onto the grill plate. Place a strip of foil underneath the skewers' ends to keep them from burning.
- Cook for 5 minutes on each side, for a total of 20 minutes. Remove the skewers from the grill & serve.

7.1 Prosciutto Wrapped Medjoul Dates

Preparation time: 10 minutes

Cooking time: 5 minutes

Servings: 8

Ingredients

- Twenty-four medjoul dates
- Salted cashews, as needed
- Eight oz prosciutto
- Two tbsp olive oil
- Juice & zest of two limes
- Flake salt, for serving
- Honey, for serving

Steps

- Set the grill temp to 400°F, then keep the lid closed for 15 minutes.
- Cut off a slit lengthways through of every date. Remove the pit & replace with one or two cashews. Press the dates to close the slit.
- Divide the prosciutto into 24 slices. Roll each date in a prosciutto slice & secure with a toothpick.
- Brush the dates with olive oil & arrange them directly on the grill grate. Cook for 5 minutes, until the prosciutto is crispy.
- Remove the dates from the grill & arrange them in a big serving platter. Squeeze lime juice over the dates & sprinkle with salt & lime zest. Drizzle some honey, a little more olive oil & serve.

7.2 Dried Cranberry Patties

Preparation time: 25 minutes

Cooking time: 5 minutes

Servings: 6

Ingredients

- Two tbsp olive oil
- One red onion, chopped
- Salt, to taste
- 2 lbs. ground pork
- Half cup dried cranberries
- 2 tbsp fennel seeds
- 2 tsp rosemary
- One egg, beaten
- Zest of half lemon
- Half tsp black pepper

Steps

- Heat the oil in a pan over medium-high heat. Add the onions, a pinch of salt & stir-fry for 5 minutes, until wilted. Remove from the heat.
- Combine the remaining ingredients in a mixing bowl. Add the onions & knead with your hands to mix. Cover with cling film & refrigerate overnight.
- Set the grill temp to 325°F, then keep the lid closed for 15 minutes.
- Remove the seasoned meat from the fridge & shape into eighteen patties.
- Arrange the patties directly onto the grill grate & cook for two to three minutes per side or until the pork is thoroughly cooked. Remove from the grill & serve.

7.3 Honey Mustard Pork Loin

Preparation time: 10 minutes

Cooking time: 1 hour

Servings: 6

Ingredients

- One pork loin, around 3 lbs.
- One onion, chopped
- Two garlic cloves, chopped
- One beer bottle
- Four tbsp honey
- 2 tsp french mustard
- One tsp cumin seeds
- One tsp dried thyme
- One tsp kosher salt
- One tsp black pepper
- Two tbsp pork rub

Steps

- Place the pork, onion, & garlic in a big resealable bag.
- Prepare the marinade. Mix in a bowl the beer, honey, mustard, cumin seeds, thyme, salt, & pepper. Pour the marinade over the pork loin & close the bag.
- Refrigerate the pork loin overnight, flipping the bag a couple of times.
- Remove the pork from the marinade & season with the por rub. Pour the marinade in an ovenproof saucepan.
- Heat the marinade on medium-high heat, bring to a boil & reduce by half.
- Set the grill temp to 350°F, then keep the lid closed for 15 minutes.
- Transfer the pan to the grill grates. Place the pork loin in the pan, fat side up. Cook the pork for around 1 hour, basting 2 or 3 times with the reduced marinade, until the pork's internal temperature reaches 145°F & the meat is nicely glazed.
- Remove the pork from the grill & let rest for 10 minutes. Slice the meat & serve with the juices from the pan.

7.4 Smoked Muffuletta Sandwich

Preparation time: 1 hour

Cooking time: 2 hours

Servings: 2

Ingredients

- Half lb. mortadella loaf, unsliced
- Two ciabatta rolls
- Five oz. salami, sliced
- Four oz. mozzarella, sliced
- Four oz. provolone, sliced
- Five oz. prosciutto, sliced
- Five oz. pepperoni, sliced

Olive Salad

- One & half cup mixed olives, pitted & chopped
- Half cup roasted red pepper, chopped
- Two cloves garlic, chopped
- Three tsp capers, chopped
- One tsp fresh oregano, chopped
- Salt & pepper, to taste
- Four tbsp olive oil
- 3 tsp red wine vinegar

Steps

- Set the grill temp to 165°F, then keep the lid closed for 15 minutes.
- Place the unsliced mortadella loaf on the grill grates & close the lid. Smoke for two hours. Let cool & slice.
- Combine all the ingredients for the olive salad in a mixing bowl.
- Cut the ciabatta buns in half horizontally. Spread the olive salad equally on the upper & lower bun halves.
- Layer the ingredients on the lowest half of the bun: smoked mortadella, salami, provolone, mozzarella, pepperoni & prosciutto. Close the sandwiches & tightly wrap in cling film.

- Refrigerate for one hour to let the flavors combine. Take the sandwiches out from the fridge, discard the plastic wrap, cut in half & serve.

7.5 Bacon Wrapped Pork Loin

Preparation time: 15 minutes

Cooking time: 3 hours

Servings: 4

Ingredients

- One cup apple juice
- One tsp salt
- One tsp Worcestershire sauce
- One pork loin roast, around 3 lbs.
- Two tbsp pork rub
- Ten slices bacon

Steps

- Pour the apple juice, 4 tbsp water, salt & Worcestershire sauce in a small mixing bowl. Whisk to dissolve the salt crystals. Inject generously the meat with a meat injector.
- Sprinkle the pork rub all over the loin & massage the meat to let the flavors penetrate.
- Set the grill temp to 225°F, then keep the lid closed for 15 minutes.
- Wrap the bacon slices around the roast. Arrange the pork loin on the grill grate & smoke for 3 to 4 hours, until the internal temperature reaches 145°F.

- Transfer the pork loin to a cutting board, cover with foil & let rest for 10 minutes. Slice & serve.

7.6 Mandarin Glazed Spareribs

Preparation time: 15 minutes

Cooking time: 5 hours

Servings: 6

Ingredients

- Three racks spareribs, membranes removed
- Three tsp yellow mustard
- One tsp Worcestershire sauce
- One cup honey
- Half cup dark sugar
- Six tbsp pork rub
- Two cans Dr. Pepper
- Half cup mandarin sauce
- One tsp sesame oil
- One tbsp soy sauce
- One tsp garlic powder

Steps

- Set the grill temp to 225°F, then keep the lid closed for 15 minutes.
- Combine Worcestershire sauce & yellow mustard in a small bowl. Rub the mixture on both sides of the ribs. Smoke for 3 hours by placing directly on the grill grate.
- Remove the ribs from the grill & arrange them in an aluminum foil pan. Drizzle honey on the ribs & sprinkle with pork rub. Pour the Dr. Pepper in the pan & cover with foil. Raise the grill temperature to 275°F & cook for 2 hours.
- Remove the foil pan from the grill & set it aside. Raise the grill to 450°F. Combine the mandarin sauce, sesame oil, soy sauce, & garlic powder in a small bowl. Remove the ribs from the foil pan & glaze them with the mixture. Place the ribs back on the grill grate, meat side up, for 10 minutes. Carve as desired & serve.

7.7 Peaches & Bourbon Spareribs

Preparation time: 10 minutes

Cooking time: 5 hours

Servings: 6

Ingredients

- Four racks spareribs, membrane removes
- Four tbsp pork rub
- Une cup apple juice
- One tbsp butter
- One onion, chopped
- 2 cups peach preserves
- One cup corn syrup
- Half cup apple cider vinegar
- Half cup Bourbon whiskey
- One tbsp Worcestershire Sauce
- One tbsp ginger, grated
- One tsp dry mustard
- One clove garlic, minced

Steps

- Season both sides of the rib with pork rub. Massage the ribs to help the flavors penetrate.
- Set the grill temp to 275°F, then keep the lid closed for 15 minutes.
- Place the ribs bone side down on the grill grate & cook for 3 hours, mopping every 30 minutes with apple juice.
- In a medium saucepan over medium-high melt the butter & stir fry the onions until wilted. Add the peach preserves, vinegar, bourbon, corn syrup, & Worcestershire sauce. Also add the ginger, mustard & garlic. Cook stirring, for 15 mins or until the sauce thickens. Set the sauce aside.
- Drop the grill temperature to 165°F & smoke the ribs for 2 more hours, mopping every 30 minutes with apple juice.
- To finish, coat the ribs with the peach sauce & raise the grill temperature to 275°F for 10 minutes, to set the glaze. Remove the ribs from the grill, carve as desired & serve along with the leftover peach sauce.

7.8 Bacon Pork Rolls

Preparation time: 10 minutes

Cooking time: 25 hours

Servings: 4

Ingredients

- One pork loin roast
- Pepper & salt, to taste.
- Two tbsp pork rub
- Four slices bacon
- BBQ sauce, to taste

Steps

- Set the grill temp to 450°F, then keep the lid closed for 15 minutes.
- With a paring knife remove all the skin & fat from the pork loin. Slice the pork loin lengthwise into four long strips with a sharp knife.
- Season the pork with salt, pepper & pork rub. Layer one slice of bacon on a pork strip & start rolling tightly. Secure each roll with one or two wooden skewers.
- Place the rolls on the hot grill grates & cook for 15 minutes.
- Flip the rolls & baste with your favorite BBQ sauce. Cook for 10 minutes, flip the rolls again & baste the other side.
- Cook 2 more minutes to ser the glaze, remove from the grill & serve.

7.9 Reverse-Seared Pork Chops

Preparation time: 5 minutes

Cooking time: 45 minutes

Servings: 4

Ingredients

- Four pork chops, bone-in
- Four tbsp pork rub
- Two tsp butter

- Two sprigs thyme
- One sprig rosemary

Steps

- Set the grill temp to 180°F, then keep the lid closed for 15 minutes.
- Generously season the pork chops with pork rub. Massage the meat to help the favors penetrate.
- Place the chops on the grill grate & smoke for 30 to 40 minutes or until the internal temperature hits 130°F.
- Take the chops off the grill & set them aside to rest for 10 minutes.
- Raise the grill temperature to 500°F. Place a cast iron pan on the grill grate & keep the lid closed for 10 minutes.
- Melt the butter in the pan & add the herb sprigs. When the butter is melted, arrange the pork chops in the pan. Sear for 3 to 4 minutes on each side, until the exterior is nicely browned.
- Remove the chops from the grill, cover with foil & let rest 5 minutes. Serve.

7.10 Easy Baby Back Ribs

Preparation time: 15 minutes

Cooking time: 5 hours

Servings: 8

Ingredients

- Three baby back ribs racks
- One cup pork rub
- One cup BBQ sauce

Steps

- Peel the membrane off from the backside of the ribs.
- Season all sides of the ribs with pork rub. Massage the meat to help the flavors penetrate.
- Set the grill temp to 180°F, then keep the lid closed for 15 minutes.
- Arrange the ribs on the grill grate & smoke for 3 or 4 hours, until the interior temperature reaches 160°F.
- Raise the grill temperature to 350°F. Arrange on a sheet of heavy-duty aluminum foil a rack of ribs. Glaze with BBQ sauce & loosely close the foil. Repeat for the other racks.
- Return the wrapped ribs to the grill & cook for 45 mins, or until the internal temperature hits 200°F.
- Remove the ribs from the grill. Let rest for 20 minutes, then unwrap the foil, cut the ribs as desired & serve.

7.11 Pulled Pork Mac & Cheese

Preparation time: 20 minutes

Cooking time: 30 minutes

Servings: 6

Ingredients

- One tsp olive oil
- Half tsp salt
- One lb. elbow macaroni, uncooked
- Four cups milk
- Eight tbsp butter
- Half cup all-purpose flour
- Four cups gruyere cheese, grated
- Two cups sharp cheddar cheese, grated
- Two cups leftover pulled pork
- One pinch black pepper
- One pinch nutmeg
- Two cups Panko breadcrumbs

- Set the grill temp to 375°F, then keep the lid closed for 15 minutes. Pour the oil into a big pot of salted hot water. Cook the macaroni according to the box instructions, around 6 to 8 Mins. Drain thoroughly.
- In a saucepan, heat the milk but do not boil it.
- Melt six tablespoons butter in a separate big 4-quart pot & whisk in the flour. Cook, constantly stirring, for 2 minutes over low heat. Add the hot milk, continue whisking & simmer for another minute or two, until thickened & smooth.
- Remove the pot from the heat & stir in the gruyere, nutmeg, salt, pepper & cheddar. Stir in the cooked macaroni & pulled pork. Transfer the mixture to a baking pan.
- Mix the remaining two tablespoons of butter with the Panko breadcrumbs & sprinkle on top.
- Bake for around 30 minutes, till the sauce has thickened & the breadcrumbs have browned. Serve hot topping with BBQ sauce, to taste.

7.12 Caveman BBQ Spareribs

Preparation time: 15 minutes

Cooking time: 4 hours

Servings: 4

Ingredients

Rub

- Four tbsp kosher salt
- Two tsp black pepper
- Two tsp smoked paprika
- Two tsp garlic powder
- Two tsp onion powder
- Two tsp chipotle chili powder

Main

- Two racks spareribs, St. Louis cut

BBQ Sauce

- Two cups tomato sauce
- Half cup water
- Half cup apple cider vinegar Half Cup
- Half cup honey
- Two tsp onion powder
- Half tsp black pepper
- One tsp ground mustard
- One tsp smoked paprika

Steps

- Set the grill temp to 225°F, then keep the lid closed for 15 minutes.
- Mix all the rub ingredients in a small bowl.
- Remove the membrane from the back of the ribs & sprinkle the rub on both sides. Massage the ribs to help the flavors penetrate & let rest for 20 minutes.
- Place the ribs bone-side down on the grill grate, close the lid & cook for 4 hours or until the internal temperature hits is 200°F.
- Prepare the sauce while the ribs are grilling. Combine all the ingredients in a saucepan & heat over medium heat.
- Brush a thin coat of sauce on all sides of the ribs & grill for another 10 minutes to allow the sauce to thicken.
- Take the ribs off the grill & let rest for 10 minutes. Slice as desired & serve.

8.1 Citrus Salmon Fillets

Preparation time: 10 minutes

Cooking time: 15 minutes

Servings: 2

Ingredients

- Two tbsp butter, softened.
- Half tsp lemon zest
- One tsp lemon juice
- Two tsp fresh dill, chopped
- Salt & pepper, to taste
- Four salmon fillets, 8 oz each, skin on
- One lemon, thinly sliced

Steps

- Set the grill temp to 350°F, then keep the lid closed for 15 minutes.
- In a small bowl mix the lemon zest, salt, pepper, dill, softened butter & lemon juice together.
- Coat each fillet in the lemony butter mix. Add on top a lemon slice.
- Arrange the fillets directly on the grill grate, skin-side down. Grill for 15 minutes, for moderate-rare, or until done according to your taste. Remove from the grill & serve.

8.2 Sake Shrimps

Preparation time: 15 minutes

Cooking time: 5 minutes

Servings: 4

Ingredients

- Four lbs. jumbo shrimps
- One cup soy sauce
- One cup teriyaki sauce
- One cup japanese sake
- One cup olive oil
- One clove garlic, chopped
- One tsp ginger, grated
- One tsp chicken rub

Steps

- Shell the shrimps. Remove the heads, then cut the back lengthwise with a paring knife & remove the black veins.
- Combine the remaining ingredients in a resealable bag & mix well.
- Add the shrimps to the bag, shake to spread the flavors & refrigerate for 2-4 hours.
- Set the grill temp to 500°F, then keep the lid closed for 15 minutes.
- Remove the shrimp from the marinade, pat dry with paper towels & thread on wooden or metal skewers. Discard the marinade.
- Arrange the skewers on the grill grate directly. Close the lid & cook it for at 3 minutes.
- Flip the skewers, close the lid & cook it for 3 more minutes.
- Remove the skewers from the grill & serve.

8.3 Lemon-Herb Butter Grilled Cod

Preparation time: 10 minutes

Cooking time: 12 minutes

Servings: 2

Ingredients

- Four tbsp salted butter, softened
- Zest & juice from half lemon
- Two clove garlic, chopped
- Two tbsp mixed herbs (parsley, thyme, chives), chopped
- Two tbsp chicken rub
- Two lbs. cod fillets

Steps

- Set the grill temp to 500°F, then keep the lid closed for 15 minutes.
- Prepare the herb butter. In a small bowl combine butter, lemon juice, lemon zest, rubs, herbs, & garlic.
- Use a little butter to grease a baking pan.
- Arrange the cod fillets in the pan, in a single layer. Top with herb butter.
- Transfer the pan to the grill grates, close the lid & cook for 12-15 mins, till the fish gets cooked.
- Remove the pan from the grill, arrange the fillets on a serving platter & serve.

8.4 Grilled Rainbow Trout

Preparation time: 10 minutes

Cooking time: 20 minutes

Servings: 2

Ingredients

- Two tbsp olive oil
- Two rainbow trout, gutted, heads on.
- One tsp fresh dill, chopped
- One tsp fresh thyme
- One tsp kosher salt
- Half onion, sliced
- One lemon, thinly sliced
- One tsp black pepper

Steps

- Set the grill temp to 400°F, then keep the lid closed for 15 minutes.
- Grease a baking dish with one tbsp olive oil.
- Arrange the trout in the baking dish & coat with the leftover olive oil.
- Season the fish with salt, dill, & thyme, inside & outside.
- Stuff the fish with lemon & onion slices, then spread some pepper on top. Also, place a slice of lemon on each fish.
- Transfer the baking dish to the grill grates, close the lid & cook for around 20 minutes, until the fish flakes using a fork. Remove from the grill & serve.

8.5 Sweet & Spicy Thai Salmon

Preparation time: 20 minutes

Cooking time: 15 minutes

Servings: 4

Ingredients

- Four tbsp soy sauce
- Two tbsp dark sugar
- One tbsp lime juice
- One tbsp Sriracha sauce
- One tbsp ginger, grated
- One tbsp garlic, minced
- One tsp chicken rub
- Half tsp sesame oil
- Four salmon fillets, skin-on
- Two tbsp scallions, chopped
- Two tbsp sesame seeds

- In a resealable plastic bag combine the soy sauce, dark sugar, sriracha, lime juice, garlic, sesame oil & ginger. Add the salmon fillets to the bag & massage to spread the flavors. Refrigerate for 1 hour, then remove the fillets from the marinade & pat dry with paper towels. Discard the marinade.
- Set the grill temp to 450°F, then keep the lid closed for 15 minutes.
- Arrange the salmon fillets directly on the grill grate, skin side down. Grill for 8-10 mins for medium doneness.
- Remove the salmon from the grill grate, sprinkle with sesame seeds, chopped scallions & serve with rice or grilled vegetables.

8.6 Smoked Sea Bass

Preparation time: 5 minutes

Cooking time: 40 minutes

Servings: 4

Ingredients

Marinade

- Four tbsp olive oil
- Juice of one lemon
- One clove garlic, chopped
- One tbsp fresh oregano
- One tsp chicken rub
- One tbsp fresh thyme

Main

- Four sea bass fillets, skin on
- Eight tbsp butter
- Two tbsp chicken rub
- Four lemon slices, for garnish

Steps

- Prepare the marinade. Combine all the marinade ingredients in a resealable bag & shake.

- Add the sea bass fillets to the bag, massage to help the flavor spreads & refrigerate for 2 hours, flipping the bag once.
- Set the grill temp to 325°F, then keep the lid closed for 15 minutes.
- Put the butter in a baking dish & place it on the grill to melt the butter.
- Remove the fish from the bag. Pour the marinade into the baking dish with the butter. Sprinkle chicken on the fish fillets.
- Arrange the fillets in the pan with the butter mixture. Cook for about 30 minutes, basting the fillets with the hot butter mixture once or twice.
- Once the internal temperature of the fish hits 160°F, remove the pan from the grill. Garnish with lemon slices & serve.

8.7 Grilled Shrimp Cocktail

Preparation time: 5 minutes

Cooking time: 10 minutes

Servings: 2

Ingredients

Main

- Two lbs. shrimps, deveined, tails on
- Two tbsp olive oil
- One tsp Old Bay seasoning
- Parsley, chopped, for garnish

Cocktail Sauce

- Half cup ketchup
- Two tsp horseradish
- One tbsp lemon juice
- Salt & pepper, to taste
- Tabasco sauce, to taste

Steps

- Set the grill temp to 350°F, then keep the lid closed for 15 minutes.
- Rinse the shrimps & pat dry with paper towels. Combine the shrimps, Old Bay seasoning & oil in a mixing bowl. Toss to

coat the shrimps, then move to a grill-safe baking dish.

- Transfer the baking dish to the grill grates & cook for 5-7 mins, or until the shrimp are opaque.
- Prepare the cocktail sauce. In a bowl mix ketchup, lemon juice, & horseradish. Season with salt & pepper to taste. Add Tabasco sauce to taste.
- Arrange the grilled shrimp in a bowl with the cocktail sauce. Sprinkle with chopped parsley & serve.

8.8 Grilled Salmon with Smoked Guacamole

Preparation time: 10 minutes

Cooking time: 30 minutes

Servings: 6

Ingredients

Main

- One tbsp fish rub
- One whole salmon fillet, around three lbs.

Guacamole

- Three avocados
- Half red onion, chopped
- Two cloves garlic, chopped
- One jalapeño pepper, chopped
- Four tbsp cilantro, chopped
- Juice of one lime
- One tsp salt
- One tbsp olive oil

Steps

- Set the grill temp to 165°F, then keep the lid closed for 15 minutes.
- Half & pit the avocadoes & arrange them cut side up on the grill grate. Smoke for 10 minutes, remove from the grill & set aside to cool.
- Raise the grill temp to 450°F, then keep the lid closed for 15 minutes.
- Arrange the salmon directly on the grill & cook for 15-20 mins, until the internal temperature of the thickest part of the salmon hits 155°F.
- In the meanwhile, prepare the guacamole. Dice the smoked avocados, place in a bowl, mash with a fork & mix with all the remaining ingredients.
- Transfer the salmon to a serving platter & serve along with the smoked guacamole.

8.9 Bacon Grilled Shrimps

Preparation time: 20 minutes

Cooking time: 20 minutes

Servings: 6

Ingredients

- One lb. extra-large shrimps
- Six whole jalapeño peppers
- Eight oz Monterey Jack cheese.
- One lb. bacon, sliced
- Two tbsp chicken rub

Steps

- Shell & devein the shrimps. Cut the shrimps back lengthwise, butterfly them & set aside. Cut the jalapenos into thin slivers. Also cut the cheese into slivers of the same size. Cut in half the bacon slices.
- Stuff each shrimp with a jalapeno slice & a cheese slice. Wrap the shrimps in a half bacon slice & secure with a toothpick.

- Season the wrapped shrimps with chicken rub.
- Set the grill temp to 425°F, then keep the lid closed for 15 minutes.
- Arrange the shrimps directly on the grill grates. Cook for about 20 minutes, rotating once, until the bacon is crispy.
- Remove the shrimps from the grill, set them aside for 10 mins to cool & serve.

8.10 Simple Grilled Tuna

Preparation time: 10 minutes

Cooking time: 10 minutes

Servings: 2

Ingredients

- One cup soy sauce
- Four tbsp olive oil
- One tbsp garlic, minced
- Juice of two lemons
- One handful basil leaves
- Two lbs. tuna fillets

Steps

- Prepare the marinade. Place in a resealable bag the soy sauce, olive oil, garlic, lemon juice, basil leaves.
- Add the tuna fillets to the bag. Massage the bag to help the flavors combine & refrigerate for 45 minutes, turning once.
- Set the grill temp to 350°F, then keep the lid closed for 15 minutes.
- Arrange the marinated tuna fillets directly on the grill grate. Grill for 5 minutes, turn the fillets & cook for more 5 minutes or until the internal temperature hits 140°F. Serve.

8.11 Vodka Brined Salmon

Preparation time: 15 minutes

Cooking time: 80 minutes

Servings: 4

Ingredients

Brine

- One cup brown sugar
- One tbsp black pepper
- Half cup coarse salt
- One cup Vodka

Main

- One whole salmon fillet, around 2 lbs.
- Lemon wedges, to serve

Steps

- Combine brown sugar, pepper, salt, & vodka in a small mixing bowl. Whisk to dissolve the salt & sugar crystals.
- Place the salmon fillet in a big resealable bag. Pour the brine over the salmon & massage to help the flavors combine. Refrigerate it for 2-4 hours.
- Remove the salmon fillet from the brine & pat dry with paper towels. Discard the brine.
- Set the grill temp to 180°F, then keep the lid closed for 15 minutes.
- Arrange the salmon fillet on the grill grate, skin side down, & smoke for 30 minutes.
- Increase the grill temperature to 225°F & cook the salmon for another 45-60 minutes, or until the internal temperature hits 140°F & the fish flakes easily with fork.
- Remove the salmon from the grill & serve with lemon wedges.

8.12 Grilled Swordfish with Salsa

Preparation time: 15 minutes

Cooking time: 30 minutes

Servings: 4

Ingredients

- Four corn ears, husked
- Four tbsp olive oil
- Salt & pepper, to taste
- Two cups cherry tomatoes, quartered
- One red onion, chopped
- One jalapeño pepper, chopped
- Juice of one lime
- One bunch cilantro, chopped
- Four swordfish fillets

Steps

- Set the grill temperature to 500°F, then keep the lid closed for 15 minutes.
- Drizzle 2 tbsp olive oil over corn & season with salt & pepper to taste. Place the corn cobs directly on the grill grate & grill for around 12-15 mins, turning once. When the corn is lightly browned, remove & let cool.
- Remove the corn kernels & put them in a medium mixing cup. Add the cilantro, tomatoes, jalapeño, red onion & lime juice. Toss to mix & season with salt to taste.
- Brush the swordfish fillets with two tbsp olive oil & season with salt & pepper.
- Arrange the on the grill grate & cook for about 18 mins, until the fish is cooked & flakes easily with a fork.
- Serve the grilled swordfish topping with corn salsa.

9.1 Chocolate Brownie Cookies

Preparation time: 15 minutes

Cooking time: 12 minutes

Servings: 6

Ingredients

- One 16 oz bittersweet chocolate bar, chopped
- Four tbsp butter
- Four eggs
- One cup sugar
- One tsp vanilla extract
- One cup flour
- Half tsp baking powder
- One cup semisweet chocolate chips

Steps

- Set the grill temperature to 350°F, then keep the lid closed for 15 minutes.
- Line up two cookie sheets with parchment paper
- In a heatproof dish mix the finely sliced chocolate & butter; place over a pan of simmering water & stir regularly until the chocolate is fully molten & smooth. Let cool.
- In a mixing bowl whisk together the sugar, eggs, & vanilla extract.
- With a rubber spatula whisk the molten chocolate mixture into the egg mixture until it is perfectly mixed.
- Add gradually flour & baking powder into the batter. Stir in the chocolate chips & mix until combined.
- Scoop tsps of dough onto the lined baking sheets. Transfer to the grill grate, close the lid & bake for 10-12 minutes, till the exterior is firm. Don't overcook.
- Remove the baking sheets from the grill. Let fully cool & serve.

9.2 Gingerbread cookies

Preparation time: 15 minutes

Cooking time: 10 minutes

Servings: 8

Ingredients

- Three quarters cup flour
- Half tsp baking soda
- Half tsp ground cinnamon
- One pinch kosher salt
- Half tsp ground ginger
- One pinch ground cloves
- One third dark sugar
- Half cup plus four tbsp sugar
- Three quarters cup butter, softened
- One egg
- Four tbsp molasses

Steps

- Set the grill temperature to 325°F, then keep the lid closed for 15 minutes.
- Combine the baking soda, flour, salt, cinnamon, cloves & ginger in a mixing bowl.
- Place the sugar (half cup), brown sugar & butter in the bowl of a stand mixer & process until light & fluffy. Add the molasses & egg & continue processing at medium speed, scraping down the bowl sides with a spatula, as required.

- Add the dry ingredients & blend at low speed until well mixed. Scrap down the sides of the bowl & blend for another 30 seconds.
- Roll tbsps of dough into balls. Roll the balls in the remaining 4 tbsp of sugar.
- Line up a cookie sheet with parchment paper. Place the dough balls on the sheet, taking care not to overcrowd.
- Cook for about 10 minutes, till lightly browned but still soft in the center.
- Remove the sheet from the grill & let cool. Serve.

9.3 Grilled Fruit with Berries & Cream

Preparation time: 15 minutes

Cooking time: 10 minutes

Servings: 4

Ingredients

- Two peaches, halved
- Two apricots, halved
- Two nectarines, halved
- Half cup balsamic vinegar
- Three tbsp honey
- One tbsp orange zest
- Two cups cream
- Half cup raspberries
- Half cup blueberries

Steps

- Set the grill temperature to 400°F, then keep the lid closed for 15 minutes.
- Arrange the apricots, nectarines, & peaches directly on the hot grill grate, 3-4 minutes per side, until nice grill marks show.
- Prepare the balsamic reduction. Place the balsamic vinegar, 2 tbsp honey & the orange zest into pan over low heat. Bring to a simmer & cook until thickened to a medium consistency.
- Meanwhile, whip the cream along with 1 tbsp of honey, until soft peaks form.
- Arrange the grilled fruit halves on a serving dish, top with berries & drizzle with balsamic reduction. Serve along with whipped cream.

9.4 Bourbon & Apple Dutch Baby

Preparation time: 20 minutes

Cooking time: 30 minutes

Servings: 4

Ingredients

- Two apples, cored & sliced
- Two oz Bourbon whiskey
- Half cup dark sugar
- One stick butter, divided
- two tsp ground cinnamon
- Three eggs
- Two thirds flour
- Half cup white sugar
- Three quarters cup milk

Steps

- Set the grill temperature to 400°F, then keep the lid closed for 15 minutes.
- Blend eggs, milk, cinnamon, flour & white sugar in a food processor. Process till absolutely smooth.
- Reserve 4 tbsp of butter. Melt the leftover butter in a saucepan pan over low heat. Add the apple slices & cook 5 minutes. Add the brown sugar & Bourbon whiskey & keep cooking cook till saucy.
- Once the grill is hot, place an ovenproof pan on the grill grates. Add 4 tsp butter & melt, greasing all the pan. Pour the egg mixture in the pan & cook for 20 mins, then reduce the grill temperature to 300°F & cook for another 5 mins, or until golden & puffy.
- Serve immediately the dutch baby topped with apples.

9.5 Christmas Shortbread Cookies

Preparation time: 12 minutes

Cooking time: 45 minutes

Servings: 24

Ingredients

- One cup butter, softened
- Four tbsp corn starch
- Three quarters cup flour
- Few drops peppermint extract
- Two cups powdered sugar
- One tsp vanilla extract
- Four tbsp milk

Steps

- Line two cookie sheets with parchment paper.
- Place the soft butter in a mixing bowl. Work with a wooden spatula until nice & smooth. Add the sugar & vanilla extract. Stir together till fluffy & properly mixed.
- Add flour & cornstarch. Stir till flour is incorporated. Transfer the dough to a lightly floured surface & press into a ball.
- With a rolling pin dusted with flour roll the dough to a half inch thickness. Cut the desired shapes & put them onto the cookie sheets. Re-roll every scrape till all the dough gets used up.
- Refrigerate the cookies for one hour or more.
- Set the grill temperature to 350°F, then keep the lid closed for 15 minutes. Bake the cookies for 12 to 14 minutes, till just starting to turn gold at edges. Set aside & let cool.
- Prepare the mint glaze. Mix the milk, peppermint extract & powdered sugar in a bowl. Mix until smooth.
- Glaze the cookies. Dip the top surface of the cookie into the glaze. Allow extra glaze to drip back into the bowl. Quickly flip the cookie right side up. Allow the glaze to dry for 15-30 minutes & serve.

9.6 Bacon Donuts

Preparation time: 15 minutes

Cooking time: 25 minutes

Servings: 12

Ingredients

- One & half cup powdered sugar
- Four tbsp maple syrup
- Two tbsp maple extract
- Two tbsp heavy cream
- Twelve glazed donuts
- Twelve strips bacon

Steps

- Set the grill temperature to 500°F, then keep the lid closed for 15 minutes.
- Combine the syrup, powdered sugar, & maple extract in a medium saucepan & bring to a boil over low heat. Simmer for 3-5 mins, stirring regularly.
- Reduce the heat to low & stir in the cream. Add more powdered sugar to achieve the perfect texture, if needed.
- Arrange the bacon strips on the grill grates. Cook it for about 5-7 mins on each side, until crispy.
- Transfer the bacon to a plate. Let cool & crumble.
- Arrange the doughnuts on the grill grates, glaze side up. Grill for 3-5 mins or until the glaze is bubbly & the doughnuts show grill marks.
- Transfer the hot doughnuts to a serving plate. Immediately drizzle with glaze & top with crumbled bacon. Serve.

9.7 Leftover Donut Pudding

Preparation time: 15 minutes

Cooking time: 40 minutes

Servings: 8

Ingredients

- Sixteen cake donuts
- Half cup raisins
- Five eggs
- Three quarters cup sugar
- Two cups heavy cream
- Two tbsp vanilla extract
- One tsp ground cinnamon
- Three quarters cup butter, melted
- Ice cream, for serving

Steps

- Butter a 9x13-inch baking pan. Chop the donuts & arrange in the pan, in a single layer. Scatter the raisins on top & drizzle with more butter
- Prepare the custard. Whisk the eggs, sugar, milk, cinnamon & vanilla in a big mixing bowl. Add the butter & whisk to combine. Pour the custard over the donuts. Let rest for 15 minutes, pressing the donuts down in the custard. Cover with foil.
- Set the grill temperature to 350°F, then keep the lid closed for 15 minutes.
- Bake for 30 - 40 minutes, till the custard is set. Remove the foil & bake for another 10 mins to lightly brown the surface.
- Allow to cool for a few minutes before cutting in squares. Serve along with ice cream.

9.8 Bacon Salted Caramel Brownies

Preparation time: 10 minutes

Cooking time: 40 minutes

Servings: 8

Ingredients

- Eight strips bacon
- Half cup kosher salt
- One brownie mix package
- One jar caramel sauce

Steps

- Set the grill temperature to 350°F, then keep the lid closed for 15 minutes.
- Prepare the bacon salt. Grill the bacon strips until very crisp, around 25 minutes. Let cool & grind in a food processor. In a small bowl, add half cup kosher salt & the crumbled bacon. If not using immediately, store the bacon salt in a jar in the refrigerator.
- Prepare the brownies mix accordingly to the box directions. Pout the mix in a buttered baking pan. Drizzle caramel sauce over the brownie batter. Sprinkle 1 tsp of bacon salt on top.
- Transfer the baking pan to the grill grate, close the lid & bake brownies for about 20-25 minutes, until the batter starts to firm up. Drizzle with 2 tsps more caramel sauce & add pinch more of bacon salt. Return the brownies to the grill for another 20-25 minutes, until toothpick insert in the middle comes out clean.
- Drizzle a last layer of caramel sauce on top of the hot brownies & some more bacon salt, if desired. Let cool before cutting brownies into squares. Serve.

9.9 Blueberry Cobbler

Preparation time: 10 minutes

Cooking time: 40 minutes

Servings: 8

Ingredients

- Four cups blueberries
- Three quarters cup sugar
- One cup orange juice

- Two thirds cup flour
- One tsp baking powder
- One pinch salt
- Half cup butter, softened
- One tbsp dark sugar

Steps

- Set the grill temperature to 350°F, then keep the lid closed for 15 minutes.
- Combine the blueberries, 4 tbsp sugar & the orange juice in a 10-inch cast iron pan.
- Combine the baking powder, flour & salt in a small mixing cup.
- Mix the butter & leftover sugar together in a separate bowl. Mix in the egg & vanilla extract. Gradually add the flour mis & thoroughly combine.
- Pour the batter over the blueberries & sprinkle with raw sugar.
- Transfer the pan to the grill grate, close the lid & bake the cobbler for 35-45 mins. Let cool slightly & serve with whipped cream.

9.10 Baked Chocolate Cake

Preparation time: 20 minutes

Cooking time: 20 minutes

Servings: 4

Ingredients

- Flour, as needed
- Four oz butter
- Six oz bittersweet chocolate
- Two eggs
- Two egg yolks
- Half cup sugar
- One pinch salt.
- Maple ice cream, to serve
- Crumbled bacon, to serve

Steps

- Set the grill temperature to 450°F, then keep the lid closed for 15 minutes.
- Butter & flour 4 6-ounce ramekins. Remove the excess flour. Place the ramekins on a baking sheet.
- On a double boiler, melt the butter & chocolate over low heat. In a mixing bowl,

whisk together the eggs, yolks, sugar, & salt until thick & creamy.
- Stir in the chocolate & whisk. Gradually add the flour & whisk to thoroughly combine.
- Divide the mixture between the ramekins & bake for 20 mins, until the sides are firm but the core still moist.
- Let cool for 1 minute. Flip each ramequin on a dessert dish to unmold the cakes.
- Sprinkle the cakes with crumbled bacon & serve along with maple ice cream.

9.11 Caramelized Bourbon Pears

Preparation time: 10 minutes

Cooking time: 30 minutes

Servings: 4

Ingredients

- Three pears
- Four tbsp dark sugar
- Four tbsp Bourbon whiskey
- Two tbsp butter, melted
- One tsp vanilla extract
- Half tsp salt
- Vanilla ice cream, to serve

Steps

- Set the grill temperature to 325°F, then keep the lid closed for 15 minutes.
- Peel & core the pears. Quarter & arrange in a buttered baking dish

- Mix in a bowl the bourbon, dark sugar, vanilla, butter, cinnamon & salt. Pour the mixture over the pears.
- Transfer the baking dish on grill grate, close the lid & bake for 30 - 35 mins, until the pears are tender.
- Arrange the pears on a serving plate & drizzle with the caramelized juices from the pan.
- Serve with vanilla ice cream while still warm.

9.12 Smokey Whipped Cream

Preparation time: 5 minutes

Cooking time: 20 minutes

Servings: 4

Ingredients

- Three cups heavy cream
- Half cup sour cream
- Six tbsp powdered sugar
- Half tbsp vanilla extract
- Fresh fruit, to serve

Steps

- Set the grill temperature to 180°F, then keep the lid closed for 15 minutes.
- Pour the heavy cream in an oven-safe bowl
- Transfer the bowl on the grill grate, close the lid & smoke for 20 minutes or more, for a stronger smoke flavor.
- Remove the pan from the grill. Let cool to room temperature & refrigerate for about 6 hours.
- Combine all the other ingredients in a mixing bowl. Fold in the smoked cream & whisk with a hand mixer until rigid peaks form.
- Serve with fresh fruit or with your favorite desserts.